PEER MEDIATION

Conflict Resolution in Schools

PROGRAM GUIDE

D1306985

Fred Schrumpf
Donna Crawford
H. Chu Usadel

Research Press Company
2612 North Mattis Avenue
Champaign, Illinois 61821

Cover design by Jack W. Davis
Composition by Wadley Graphix Corporation
Printed by Malloy Lithographing

ISBN 0–87822–330–4

Library of Congress Catalog No. 91–62575

To Gabe, Anneke, Vincent, and Michael—may they create peaceful resolutions

Contents

Figures

Acknowledgments

This book began with a commitment to a vision of peace and our awareness of the educator's responsibility for creating an environment where students can learn to understand and accept their connection to the world around them. Support and ideas seemed to emerge from everywhere. Many individuals along the way were willing to blend their energies with ours; we believe this combined energy truly strengthened our ability to create. We are grateful to all.

We appreciate the opportunities we have encountered in our community and in our school system. We especially wish to acknowledge the following individuals for their involvement: Dr. James Roland and Dr. Henry Meares, for allowing us the freedom to be risk-takers; Jefferson Humphrey, for his personal support and illuminating participation; Norman Baxley, for his generosity and inspiration; Katie Bridges, for her efforts and commitment to the vision; and Ken Waltsgott, for facilitating community and financial support for peer mediation programs.

Then there are our teachers. Edith Primm, Charles Crowley, Al Smith, and Suzanne Miller are true learning facilitators who exemplify quality conflict resolution training. We have learned much from their wisdom. Special recognition goes to Dina Davis and Mike Kotner for being great mentors and spiritual friends—their gifts are significant. We also deeply appreciate all that we have learned from our students. Each, often unknowingly, has helped us develop and refine our ideas.

Without Robin Odeh's willingness to spend her Saturdays, Sundays, and evenings word processing our endless series of drafts, this book would never have met the deadline. Thank you, Robin, for your effort and patience. We are also thankful to Karen Steiner, our editor, for her insights and dedication to clarity.

Finally, we are grateful for the support and understanding of Golie Jansen, Richard Bodine, and Morgan Usadel, who were compelled to endure a certain amount of disharmony and conflict so that this book could be written.

Introduction

When students bring their conflicts to teachers, teachers most typically respond by advising them to "ignore it" or "walk away." When students bring their conflicts to their friends, the response is often "get 'em back." If conflicts reach the principal's attention, detention or suspension is often the result. None of these common responses resolves the conflicts. In fact, some of these strategies can actually increase conflicts.

To coexist peacefully, students need skills to express their needs and wants adequately and to create boundaries for themselves in a responsible manner. This Program Guide and the Student Manual that accompanies it describe our attempt to help middle and high school students acquire these skills and deal with school-based conflict through peer mediation. Our program, Common Ground, was first implemented at the secondary level in Urbana, Illinois. In 3 years of operation at Urbana Middle School, over 500 disputes were resolved at a 95 percent success rate. The model has also been adopted in several other school districts across the Midwest and has been used successfully to resolve a variety of conflicts. Many of these conflicts started with arguing and name-calling and had the potential to lead to violence. Other more common conflicts stimulating requests for mediation came from students who had been threatened, who had been the victim of rumors, or who had property lost or damaged.

The information necessary for conducting a successful peer mediation program is included in this volume and the Student Manual: background information on the nature of conflict, an overview of the peer mediation process, descriptions of program organization and procedures, and training activities and materials.

WHAT IS PEER MEDIATION?

The peer mediation approach presented here assumes that conflict is a normal and positive force that can accompany personal growth and social change. To deal with conflict, a trained peer mediator facilitates a process of communication and problem solving that leads to resolution. Peer mediation is explained to students as "a chance to sit face to face and talk, uninterrupted, so each side of the dispute is heard. After the problem is defined, solutions are created and then evaluated. When an agreement is reached, it is written and signed."

When conflicts arise, most people either react with verbal or physical aggression, ignore the situation, or withdraw from it and blame themselves. Unresolved conflicts often result in hurt feelings, loss of friends, increased anger or frustration, and sometimes physical violence. Considering the competitive nature of our society, it is not surprising that conflicts become contests where there must be a winner and a loser. This win/lose attitude is a separate and disconnected view of society.

Peer mediation redefines conflicts in such a way that no one has to lose. It is a commitment to cooperate and create new possibilities beneficial to all involved. In looking for a common solution, disputants become partners and share in a dialogue about the quality of their lives. In addition, peer mediation teaches democratic principles and offers a forum through which students can participate in their school community. Thus, it can become a voice for those who feel alienated or underrepresented, creating social consciousness and empowering participants through responsible social action.

The specific benefits of peer mediation are as follows.

1. Peer mediation teaches students to see conflict as a part of everyday life and an opportunity to grow and learn.

2. Peer mediation can be more effective than suspension or detention in teaching responsible behavior.

3. Peer mediation can help reduce violence, vandalism, and absenteeism in schools.

4. Peer mediation reduces the time teachers and administrators deal with discipline.

5. Peer mediation is a life skill that empowers students to solve their own problems through improved communication, problem solving, and critical thinking.

6. Peer mediation promotes mutual understanding of various individuals and groups throughout the school community.

PEER MEDIATION AS LEADERSHIP DEVELOPMENT

"Students helping students" is an important concept in the secondary schools that finds expression in peer counseling and/or peer leadership. But, due to the increasing complexity of the social and emotional problems that today's teenagers experience, the sponsors of peer helping programs often find themselves faced with increased liability.

Peer mediation differs from other peer helping programs in that the mediators are taught to handle a clearly defined, formal process. They act as facilitators between two peer disputants. They do not take sides, give advice, or assume responsibility for solving the dispute. They are trained only to assist those in conflict to solve their own problem.

Peer mediation can be introduced or added to a currently established student leadership or helping program. In doing so, a school can extend its services to improve the atmosphere of the whole school community. Generally, a program that offers a better alternative to resolving school conflicts has no difficulty finding enthusiastic support from school staff.

Specific life skills like self-control, communication, problem solving, critical thinking, and planning form the basis of the mediation process. These are skills that all students need to learn. Students who participate in mediation feel an increased sense of internal control and positive self-esteem. There is no lack of motivation when peer mediators confront real-life problem situations.

Creating a school with a healthy climate is a major challenge for students, teachers, and administrators, and the way a school community handles conflicts can have a profound effect on the overall school climate. A healthy school community will use conflict to teach important life skills that promote peace and fairness. It accomplishes this by helping students develop a respectful sensitivity toward individual differences in our multicultural world. Peer mediation can play an important part in developing this sensitivity.

CHAPTER 1

Understanding Conflict

Conflict is a natural, vital part of life. When conflict is truly understood, it can become an opportunity to learn and create. The synergy of conflict can create new alternatives—something that was not possible before. Examples of such synergy exist everywhere in nature: In the forest, the nutrients provided by decaying leaves support the growth of enormous trees. In the sea, a beautiful pearl is the synergistic result of sand irritating a sensitive oyster inside its shell.

The challenge for people in conflict is to apply the principles of creative cooperation that can be learned from nature in their human relationships. When differences are acknowledged and appreciated—and when the conflicting parties build on one another's strengths—a climate is created that nurtures the self-worth of each individual and provides opportunities for fulfillment to each.

PERCEPTIONS OF CONFLICT

Without conflict, there would likely be no personal growth or social change. Unfortunately, when it comes to conflict the perceptions of most people are quite negative. When asked to list words or phrases associated with conflict, most adults, as well as most children, respond negatively: "Get rid of it," "It's harmful," "War," "Hate," "Get even," and so forth. These negative attitudes about conflict are likely the result of assimilated messages from the media, parents, teachers, friends, government officials, and most others with whom one encounters conflict.

Negative perceptions and the reactions they provoke are extremely detrimental to successful conflict resolution. However, before they can be replaced, they must first be understood. To start, think about your own attitudes toward conflict: Does denying the existence of conflict help you resolve it? Does accusing or defending help you to cooperate? Can you make a conflict go away by not thinking about it? Are you really able to force another person to change? Does assuming there will be a winner and loser help?

The answers to these questions reveal that everyone in every conflict has a choice—to be driven by negative perceptions or to take control of the situation and act in a positive way. With more personal awareness and better understanding of available choices, one becomes able to approach conflict knowing that it can have either destructive or constructive results. When conflict is perceived as a positive life force, those in conflict become responsible for producing a result in which relationships are enhanced and individuals are empowered to control their own lives in ways that respect the needs of others. In brief, the power to create resolution lies within each person.

It is important to realize that students' success in developing an awareness of the positive potential of conflict is an outgrowth of their teachers' own endeavors and commitment to approach conflict in a positive way. Teachers who model positive ways of resolving conflict in school will see results that have a powerful effect on their own lives and work, as well as on the lives and work of their students.

ORIGIN OF CONFLICT

As Dr. William Glasser explains, conflict originates within: We are not controlled by external events but instead are motivated by the desire to satisfy certain needs that exist internally.* Simply, these are genetic instructions that we must follow if we are to grow. Glasser explains that some of these genetic instructions are satisfied psychologically rather than physically. He believes that individuals are all driven by the following four psychological needs.

1. The need to *belong*—loving, sharing, and cooperating with others

2. The need for *power*—achieving, accomplishing, and being recognized and respected

3. The need for *freedom*—making choices in our lives

4. The need for *fun*—laughing and playing

These needs seem to conflict with one another, and the constant challenge to satisfy them requires continual renegotiation of balance. For example, when a person chooses to work long hours, his accomplishments may help to meet his power need but he may not be involved with his friends and family in a need-fulfilling way. Perhaps another individual derives a sense of freedom from living alone but loses a sense of belonging when exercising this choice. Everyone knows a golfer who struggles to balance the need for fun and the need for belonging, met by spending time on weekends with family.

Each individual pictures differently the things that he or she believes will satisfy these needs. Glasser refers to the place in the mind where one stores these pictures as the *personal picture album*. The personal picture album contains detailed images of what we want. We have a number of pictures for every need; anything that satisfies a need is stored in the picture album. Our lives are spent enlarging this album.

Even though all people are driven by the same four needs, each person's wants—or pictures—are unique. It is impossible for two people to have the same picture album because it is impossible for two people to live exactly the same life. If a person wishes to understand conflict and perceive it positively, the knowledge that no two people can have exactly the same wants is central. If two individuals wish to satisfy their need to belong through a friendship, they must learn to share their commonalities and respect and value their differences.

As long as people have conflicting wants and as long as an individual's needs can be satisfied in ways that may conflict, the need to

---

* The following discussion has been drawn largely from William Glasser's book *Control Theory*. This work and others by Dr. Glasser are referenced in the bibliography.

renegotiate balance will persist. Thus, driven by our genetic instructions, we will inevitably experience conflict.

Diagnosing the source of a conflict can help define a problem, and a definition of the problem is the starting point in any attempt to find a solution. Almost every conflict involves an endeavor by the disputants to meet the basic psychological needs for belonging, power, freedom, and fun. Limited resources and different values may appear to be the cause of conflicts, but unmet needs are truly at their root.

Unmet Psychological Needs

Conflict resolution is next to impossible as long as one side believes its psychological needs are being threatened by the other. Unless unmet needs are expressed, the conflict will often reappear even when a solution is reached regarding the subject of the dispute. In short, psychological needs are satisfied by people rather than by things.

Limited Resources

Conflicts involving limited resources (time, money, property) are typically the easiest to resolve. People quickly learn that cooperating instead of competing for scarce resources is in their best interests. In cooperation, disputants share in problem solving, recognize each other's interests, and create choices. This process usually provides satisfaction because the psychological needs of belonging and power, perhaps even of freedom and fun, are addressed in the equitable allocation of limited resources.

It is important to realize how conflicts over unmet psychological needs are played out against the backdrop of limited resources. For instance, the student who is upset over the fact that his friend has not repaid a loan may really want to know his friend respects him (a power need). He may not easily accept a payment solution unless his need for recognition is addressed in the process.

Different Values

Conflicts involving different values (convictions, priorities, principles) tend to be the most difficult to resolve. When a person holds a value, he or she has an enduring belief that a specific action or quality is preferable to an opposite action or quality. This belief applies to attitudes toward objects, situations, or individuals. The belief becomes a standard that guides the person's actions.

When the terminology used to express a conflict includes words such as *honest, equal, right,* and *fair,* the conflict is typically one of values. Many times disputants think in terms of "right/wrong" or "good/bad" when values are in opposition. Even conflicts over differing goals can be viewed as value conflicts: The source of a goal conflict relates either to the goal's relative importance for each disputant or to the fact that the disputants highly value different goals.

When values are in conflict, the disputants often perceive the dispute as a personal attack. They tend to personalize the conflict because their whole sense of self feels threatened. When people feel attacked, they typically become defensive and stubbornly cling to their own convictions. Strong stances on principle are therefore characteristic of values conflicts. The conflict exists because the disputants are governed by different sets of rules. Because the disputants evaluate the problem and each other according to conflicting criteria, resolution can be especially difficult.

Again, psychological needs are enmeshed in values conflicts. For example, a person may be in conflict when a friend does not keep a promise. The person's picture of a friend is that of someone who is reliable, and her sense of belonging is threatened because her value system includes the assumption that friends do not make promises they cannot keep.

Rigid value systems can severely restrict one from meeting the need to belong. The more one adheres to any value, the more one's belonging is limited to others who hold the same beliefs. Inflexible values are also almost always destructive to our need to be free. We see others as wrong if they do not hold our beliefs, and we see situations as bad if they do not meet our standards. When this is the case, our options in life as well as our choice of friends become limited.

Resolving a values conflict does not mean the disputants must change or align their values. Often a mutual acknowledgment that each person views the situation differently is the first step toward resolution. If the disputants can learn not to reject each other because of differences in beliefs, they will be better able to deal with the problem on its own merits.

RESPONSES TO CONFLICT

Actions in response to conflict include avoidance, confrontation, and communication. These actions in turn affect the outcome of conflict.

Avoidance

People attempt to avoid conflict by withdrawing from the situation, ignoring the problem, and denying their emotions. When people choose to avoid conflict, it is usually because they have no interest in maintaining the relationship or they lack the skills to negotiate a resolution. Avoidance strategies may have some merit for the immediate situation—for example, they may help a person control anger. However, they typically result in feelings of disillusionment, self-doubt, and anxiety about the future.

Avoidance is considered a lose/win approach to conflict. People who avoid conflicts lose in the sense that they have little courage to express their own feelings and convictions and are intimidated by others. When conflicts are avoided, basic psychological needs are not acknowledged or met. Thus, people who avoid conflicts are not in effective control of their lives; they see themselves as victims, and their relationships with others invariably suffer.

Avoidance can also be a lose/lose approach to conflict when both people deny the existence of the conflict or when they will only deal with superficial issues and not the interests at the root of the problem. In either situation, neither person gets what he or she wants—in other words, they both lose.

Confrontation

Confrontation in a conflict is characterized by threats, aggression, and anger. Confrontation frequently involves bribery and punishment, the latter including withholding money, favors, and affection. Such tactics are usually viewed as being successful by the aggressor. This is a win/lose arrangement: The aggressor wins and the other person loses. Hostility and physical damage result from the win/lose mentality. In addition, this attitude is always detrimental to cooperation.

Confrontation can also be a lose/lose approach, as happens when people view someone who opposes them as "the enemy." In their desire to punish or get even, these individuals can take vindictive actions that harm themselves as well as their opponent.

Communication

Communication, fundamental to cooperative interaction, means to participate in a common understanding. People in conflict who seek first to understand, then to be understood, produce win/win results. Effective communication requires the skills of empathic listening, or listening with the intent to understand. People who are empathic listeners get inside another person's frame of reference to see the problem as that person does and to realize that person's feelings. The goal of empathic listening is not to agree; rather, it is to comprehend the person emotionally and intellectually. When people listen with empathy, they create the opportunity for each participant to meet the psychological need for power. When people are empowered, they understand they are responsible for finding their own solutions.

Effective communication in conflict is proactive, not reactive. When people use reactive language to communicate, they are attempting to transfer responsibility: "There is nothing I can do—I am not responsible" (in other words, not able to choose a response). They perceive their emotions as being governed by something outside their control. Conversely, proactive language indicates that the person takes responsibility for his or her actions and has the ability to choose a response.

When people behave proactively, they do not feel victimized and out of control; they do not blame other people or circumstances when in conflict. Instead, they take charge of their actions and feelings in a way that makes resolution possible.

Impact of Responses to Conflict

The actions people choose when they are involved in a conflict will either increase or decrease the problem: Avoidance may temporarily decrease the problem but is ineffective as a long-term strategy. Confrontation may squelch the immediate issues at the price of continued hostility. Communication offers the only possibility for a lasting solution.

When conflict escalates or remains unresolved, it can be destructive. As a conflict escalates, threats increase. More people become involved and take sides. Anger, fear, or frustration is expressed, and people become entrenched in their positions. When differences are communicated and resolution reached, conflict deescalates and threats are eliminated. People remain calm and are willing to listen to opposing viewpoints. Those involved focus on the problem rather than on each other.

In summary, then, conflict in and of itself is not positive or negative. Rather, the actions we choose turn conflict into a competitive, devastating battle or into a constructive challenge where there is opportunity for growth.

CHAPTER 2

Introduction to Peer Mediation

Peer mediation is a method for negotiating disputes and finding resolutions that combines the needs of the parties in conflict instead of compromising those needs. It is a way for students to deal with differences without coercion. Peer mediation works well to resolve conflict in schools because through it students gain power. The more students become empowered to resolve their differences peacefully, the more responsibly they behave.

Peer mediation is voluntary. Students may request mediation when they are involved in a dispute, or they may be referred by teachers, administrators, or parents. When both parties agree to mediate, an assigned peer mediator arranges a meeting with the students.

ROLE OF THE PEER MEDIATOR

The mediation process is a step-by-step method that requires flexibility and spontaneity according to each situation. The peer mediator's role throughout the process is proactive—that is, the mediator is responsible for creating and maintaining an atmosphere that fosters mutual problem solving.

Throughout a session, the mediator decides when to give more time to a person or a particular issue and what questions to ask in order to gather and use information. These decisions direct the flow of the mediation process. Thus, it is the peer mediator's role to monitor the communication between disputants constantly to maintain a balanced exchange.

In order to build trust and cooperation, the mediator works to achieve the following goals.

- ▲ *The peer-mediator is unbiased.* The mediator must be neutral and objective and avoid taking sides. In addition, he or she must be aware of any personal biases and work to keep them from distorting perceptions of people and situations.

- ▲ *The peer mediator is an empathic listener.* Effective communication skills are essential to mediation and influence each step of the process. Often the problem is clouded by issues in the relationship—emotions run high, unfounded inferences are treated as fact, and blame focuses attention on past actions. Communication skills used effectively acknowledge emotions and clarify perceptions, freeing people to understand and work on the problem.

The peer mediator uses the following communication skills throughout the process:

— Active listening, or using nonverbal behaviors to indicate that what the disputants are thinking and feeling has been understood. These nonverbal behaviors include tone of voice, eye contact, facial expressions, posture, and gestures.

— Summarizing, or restating facts by repeating the most important points, organizing interests, and discarding extraneous information. In summarizing, the mediator also acknowledges emotions by stating the feelings each person is experiencing.

— Clarifying, or using open-ended questions and statements to ensure understanding and obtain more information.

▲ *The peer mediator is respectful.* The mediator is able to treat both parties with respect and understanding, and without prejudice. Being respectful means that the mediator understands a person's emotions and beliefs. A key to respect is knowing and accepting that we are all different.

▲ *The peer mediator helps people work together.* The mediator is responsible for the process, not the solution. The solution is the responsibility of the disputants. When both parties cooperate, they are able to find their own solutions.

▲ *The peer mediator keeps information confidential.* If students are to value the process, the mediator must have the integrity to uphold confidentiality.

PREPARING FOR PEER MEDIATION

The proper physical arrangement is important for communication. Equality of equipment and positioning should be considered so that no party is at an auditory, visual, physical, or psychological disadvantage. With the proper preparations, the peer mediator demonstrates a sense of control and provides a secure climate in which the parties are able to reach an agreement.

It works best for the disputants to sit at a table at which chairs have already been arranged. The mediator instructs the parties to sit facing each other at opposite sides of the table. The mediator sits at the head of the table between the parties and preferably nearest the exit. (Having the mediator sit nearest the exit subtly discourages either party from leaving the room.)

The mediator should also carefully prepare all necessary forms before the session begins and have a pen or pencil ready for each disputant.

STEPS IN THE PEER MEDIATION PROCESS

The steps in the peer mediation process, described briefly in the following pages, are as follows.

▲ Step 1: Open the session

▲ Step 2: Gather information

▲ Step 3: Focus on common interests

▲ Step 4: Create options

▲ Step 5: Evaluate options and choose a solution

▲ Step 6: Write the agreement and close

The following summary of steps is expanded upon in the training activities presented in chapter 5. The reader will find the case example included as part of Activity 6 in that chapter an especially helpful illustration of the basic process.

Step 1: Open the Session

The peer mediator begins the session by making introductions and welcoming the disputants. The mediator then states a number of ground rules designed to the facilitate the process.

▲ Mediators remain neutral.

▲ Mediation is confidential.

▲ Interruptions are not allowed.

▲ Disputants must cooperate.

Disputants are asked individually whether they agree to abide by these ground rules.

The introduction and statement of ground rules help structure a win/win climate by establishing the goal of reaching an agreement that considers both parties' interests. The opening also begins to convey the fact that the mediator's role is to help the disputants reach their own solution to the problem. An effective opening is very important in achieving a positive outcome.

Step 2: Gather Information

The purpose of this step is to ascertain each disputant's point of view about the incident or situation. The peer mediator clarifies each party's position, finds out if the conflict is long-lasting or recent, and attempts to pinpoint any differences in values.

The mediator gathers information by first asking one disputant to tell what happened. The mediator then summarizes this disputant's story to be sure that the information has been accurately heard and that each disputant is aware of major issues and each other's perceptions. The mediator next asks the other disputant to tell what happened. Again, the mediator summarizes these statements.

The mediator then asks each disputant in turn for additional comments about the conflict and continues to do so until all the important information has been stated. As needed, the mediator seeks clarification by asking questions such as "What did you think when that happened?"; "Explain more about that"; and "What were your reasons for doing that?"

While gathering information, the mediator must validate the concerns and feelings of each disputant as well as clarify the sequence of events. When the mediator acknowledges the messages expressed and demonstrates an accurate perception of the problem, the disputants know they have been understood. This builds trust and encourages a constructive dialogue about the problem.

Step 3: Focus on Common Interests

In this crucial step, the peer mediator guides the disputants in identifying their underlying interests. Often the students in conflict are locked into rigid positions. When the mediator asks them to look behind their opposing positions, they often find that they share certain interests or that their interests, even if different, are compatible. The mediator discovers these common interests by asking such questions as "If you were in the other person's shoes, how would you feel?" and "What will be the consequences if you do not reach an agreement?"

During this questioning process, the mediator continues to listen actively by summarizing the interests of each person. It helps to make common interests explicit and to formulate them as mutual goals by saying something like "Both of you seem to agree that . . ."

Common interests serve as the building blocks for the resolution. If they are not disclosed, there is little chance of making an agreement both sides can keep. The mediator does not move on to the next step until common interests are found.

Step 4: Create Options

Creating options involves brainstorming. This brainstorming step, designed to produce as many ideas as possible, helps individuals solve problems creatively—one idea usually stimulates another. Because evaluation hinders creativity, the process of generating options is separate from the process of choosing a solution.

At this stage, then, students are not attempting to determine the best solution. Instead, they are inventing options upon which both sides can build and from which they can jointly choose in the next step of the mediation process. A lasting agreement is more likely to come from a variety of options.

To begin, the peer mediator instructs the disputants to look for solutions that will join their interests and leave both sides satisfied. The mediator next states the rules for brainstorming.

- ▲ Say any ideas that come to mind.
- ▲ Do not judge or discuss the ideas.
- ▲ Come up with as many ideas as possible.

As necessary, the mediator helps the brainstorming process along by asking questions such as "What other possibilities can you think of?" and "In the future, what could you do differently?" The mediator records the ideas on a standard form as the disputants generate them. Doing so helps stimulate other ideas and promotes cooperative problem solving. The brainstorming period is concluded after several ideas have been recorded.

Step 5: Evaluate Options and Choose a Solution

The peer mediator begins this step by asking the disputants to nominate from the list of options previously generated the ideas or parts of ideas that they think have the best possibilities of working. The mediator circles the ideas each disputant suggests.

The disputants' task at this stage is to evaluate the circled options and improve them. The mediator helps by making a number of inquiries about each option: "What are the consequences of deciding to do this?"; "Is this option a fair solution?"; "Does it address the interests of everyone involved?"; and so forth.

When the disputants come to an agreement, the mediator helps them check to see whether it is sound—in other words, whether the agreement is effective, mutually satisfying, specific, realistic, and balanced. The step ends with the mediator's summarizing all points of the agreement.

Step 6: Write the Agreement and Close

The peer mediator prepares a written statement of agreement on a standard form. This document is a brief, clear expression of the actions to which the students have agreed. The purpose of this written agreement is to influence future conduct in a way that decreases the need for further mediation. If problems arise after mediation, a well-written agreement will clarify issues and support the disputants' intentions at the time of mediation.

After the agreement is written, the mediator reads it aloud and asks if it expresses the intent of both students. The disputants and the mediator then sign the agreement. The mediator closes by shaking hands with both parties, encouraging them to shake hands with each other, and thanking them for participating in mediation.

CAUCUSING

Caucusing, or meeting with each disputant individually, is rarely necessary in peer mediation. However, it may be helpful in situations where disputants are not communicating effectively and resolution seems impossible. The caucus can be used in a number of ways.

1. To uncover information or clarify details that disputants may be willing to give only in private

2. To move beyond an impasse

3. To reduce tension between disputants

4. To explore options

5. To give people time to think alone and reflect

6. To build trust in the peer mediator

Caucusing may take place more than once and at any time during the mediation, or it may not be used at all. The peer mediator decides whether or not a caucus is necessary. When the mediator determines a caucus is necessary for one disputant, he or she maintains fairness by offering to caucus with the other disputant as well.

Before returning to the joint session, the mediator must have a clear understanding regarding what information each student does not want revealed: All statements made during caucusing are confidential unless the disputant agrees that the information may be divulged.

DEALING WITH POTENTIAL PROBLEMS

With consistent and supportive adult supervision, a peer mediation program will grow stronger as peer mediators gain experience. However, the following common problems may arise.

A Student Makes Numerous Requests for Peer Mediation

The student who repeatedly requests peer mediation could lack the social skills to have appropriate interactions with peers or could be using mediation to get out of class or obtain individual attention. If a student is requesting mediation too frequently, it would be best for an adult to handle the mediation and assess the problem.

If the student continues to submit requests, mediation sessions can be limited—perhaps to one each week. If the problem persists, it may be necessary to refer the student to the school counselor or school social worker for more specific social-emotional counseling.

More Than Two Students Request Peer Mediation

Sometimes small groups of students will request peer mediation, or perhaps a disputant will want to bring others into the session. It is best to limit the mediation to the two students who experienced the original problem. However, there will be times when others need to be involved. If more than four students must participate, it may work best for an adult and student to co-mediate the session.

Disputants Hold to Their Positions

Usually, the first 15 minutes of a session will indicate whether a resolution can be reached. When disputants appear unwilling to cooperate even when the mediation is lengthy, several options are possible. The peer mediator can try to encourage a settlement by caucusing or by asking each disputant what will likely be lost if the conflict is not resolved. If these options do not work, the mediator can ask a supervising adult to become involved. The adult can ask the participants to table the mediation until the next day and to agree to a truce until then.

No Agreement Is Reached

If an agreement is not signed, peer mediators should not feel that they have failed. Even an attempted mediation can be a positive experience because the two people in conflict have communicated their thoughts and feelings about a problem. This in itself is a step towards mutual understanding and resolution.

The Agreement Is Broken

A broken agreement usually means that the peer mediation process was incomplete, resulting in an agreement that did not reflect all the issues in the conflict. In most cases, if disputants are willing, the conflict should be brought back to the mediation table and the process continued. A second mediation will usually produce a successful resolution.

Confidentiality Is Violated

Confidentiality may be violated by either the disputants or the mediator. There is no way to keep disputants from discussing the mediation with friends; however, the peer mediator should be issued a strong warning for disclosing the names of disputants or any details of the session. If the mediator continues to breach confidentiality, he or she may lose status for a period of time or be suspended entirely from the program.

Of course, peer mediators can and should discuss sessions with other mediators or their adult supervisors. In fact, it is essential that mediators report any problems that may require referral to counseling or other adult assistance. In this way, students who need help beyond peer mediation can receive it.

CHAPTER 3

Program Organization and Implementation

This chapter describes procedures for organizing and operating a peer mediation program. The exact content and sequence of implementation will vary with each school's philosophy, available resources, needs, and size. However, the procedures described can be readily adapted for almost any school.

Figure 1 outlines four phases for developing and establishing a peer mediation program in the school. Program sponsorship and promotion are discussed in chapter 4. Procedures for implementing peer mediator training are detailed in chapters 5 and 6. All other procedures are discussed in this chapter.

CREATE AN ADVISORY COMMITTEE

Establishing a new program can begin with a small group of staff committed to the idea of peer mediation. This group may begin to organize the program by creating an advisory committee. An advisory committee that includes parent, faculty, administrator, student, and community representation is crucial to program success. This team approach builds a foundation of support for peer mediation. The responsibilities of this group may include planning long-range goals, developing proposals, planning student orientation assemblies, selecting peer mediators, organizing training sessions, developing procedures and forms, promoting the program, and assisting program coordinators with record keeping and evaluation. In addition, some committee members may participate in training peer mediators; these members should undergo the more extensive staff training program described later in this chapter.

DEVELOP A PROPOSAL

Having a brief written proposal to present to the school administration, school board, PTA, faculty, and community is extremely helpful. This proposal gives an overview of the peer mediation program, notes program goals, identifies staff involved, indicates implementation phases and the proposed timeline, and lists needed resources. The proposal can serve as a vehicle for establishing and communicating program standards and expectations. (A sample proposal is included in Appendix A.)

Figure 1 *Phases of Program Organization and Implementation*

PHASE I: Develop Involvement and Commitment

☐ Create an advisory committee (parents, faculty, administration, students, community)

☐ Develop a proposal

☐ Designate program coordinators

PHASE II: Establish School and Community Support

☐ Deliver orientation to all staff

☐ Develop resources and obtain sponsorship (see chapter 4)

☐ Establish procedures

☐ Present the program to students

☐ Select peer mediators

PHASE III: Provide Training for Trainers and Peer Mediators

☐ Provide training for trainers

☐ Conduct peer mediator training (core activities; see chapter 5)

PHASE IV: Implement Program

☐ Promote the program (see chapter 4)

☐ Provide ongoing peer mediator training and support (ongoing activities; see chapter 6)

☐ Keep records and evaluate program

DESIGNATE PROGRAM COORDINATORS

It is important to select program coordinators who understand and believe in the peer mediation process and the importance of conflict resolution. Because it will be these individuals' responsibility to carry out the proposed peer mediation program, the coordinators must also have good organizational skills.

Coordinating staff models will vary depending on the school's schedule and available staff resources. The program may be administered by a single program coordinator, if desired. Some other possible models are as follows.

▲ School social worker coordinates with school counselor.

▲ Suspension room teacher coordinates with school counselor, social worker, or administrator.

▲ Assistant principal coordinates with a teacher assigned one or two class periods each day to the program.

▲ Administrator or support services worker coordinates program; two teachers are assigned to supervise the mediation center at different times during the day.

The program coordinators' duties include, among others, facilitating meetings of an advisory committee, making assignments, keeping the project on its timeline, and supporting other committee members. Coordinators are also responsible for general supervision of peer mediators and a final program evaluation. A class period or two each day could be designated for coordinators to carry out these responsibilities. The program may be more successful if this time is established as part of the school work day.

DELIVER ORIENTATION TO ALL STAFF

The next step is for program coordinators to provide the entire school staff with an orientation to the peer mediation project. The coordinators can explain program goals, procedures, the project timeline, and methods for peer mediator selection and training. It is important for the faculty to know how creative conflict resolution improves the overall school climate. The following points are important to stress.

1. Conflict is a part of everyday life, an opportunity from which to learn and grow.

2. Peer mediation can be more effective than detention or suspension in teaching responsible behaviors.

3. Peer mediation can help reduce violence, vandalism, and absenteeism.

4. Peer mediation can reduce the time teachers, administrators, and counselors deal with discipline problems.

5. Peer mediation is a life skill that empowers students to solve their own problems through improved communication, applied decision making, and critical thinking.

6. Peer mediation promotes peace and understanding of individual differences in our multicultural world.

The peer mediation process can be demonstrated by having staff or students trained in mediation procedures role-play a session, using one of the role-play situations provided in Appendix B. Such a demonstration can help convince even skeptical staff of program value.

In addition to the orientation, a supplementary inservice training workshop will give faculty a chance to experience the mediation process more fully. Such an expanded workshop could employ selected materials used for peer mediator training (see chapters 5 and 6), as well as role-play practice in conducting mediation sessions. Beyond offering a better sense of what mediation is, these experiences will help staff learn skills they can apply in the classroom and in the school.

At the end of the orientation, an invitation can be issued for staff to participate as advisory committee members and in the training and supervision of peer mediators.

ESTABLISH PROCEDURES

It is important that every school establish simple and efficient procedures to encourage referrals and allow for a quick response. Basic operating procedures for the peer mediation center should take into account what type of conflicts the center will mediate, when mediation will take place, and how referrals will be processed. If a dispute is referred to peer mediation and the students agree to the process, the conflict is worth trying to mediate. The key is that the students agree to participate voluntarily.

Hours of Operation

The peer mediation center could be open for referrals one or more class periods each day. In some schools, where the staff might be especially concerned about students missing class time, the center could be open during homeroom, study hall, library time, lunch, or after school. A staff person should be available to assist students whenever the center is open.

The Referral Process

Peer Mediation Request forms should be readily available to students, faculty, and administrators. (A sample form is provided in Appendix C.) One way to make these forms available is to ask teachers to display in their classrooms a poster that has them attached. Forms should also be available in the school's main office and in any support service offices. It is advisable to have more than one location for the forms to be deposited. There could be a box in the main office, a box by the mediation center, and perhaps a designated locker in a central hallway. A program coordinator should check all locations daily.

Scheduling the Mediation Session

Once a mediation is requested, program coordinators should schedule it as soon as possible. Requests should not have to wait more than a day. Coordinators must use their best judgment in selecting the most appropriate peer mediator for each conflict situation. The mediator selected must be able to remain neutral; this means he or she should not be hearing the dispute of a friend. In some situations—for example, a cross-racial dispute—it may be necessary for two mediators to co-mediate.

Process for Conducting the Session

The disputants and peer mediator are called to the mediation session at a time most convenient for all. The Peer Mediator Release included in Appendix C may be helpful in assessing classroom teachers' willingness to release students from class.

When the disputants arrive, an adult supervisor should check to see whether they know the reason for the request and remind them that they are agreeing voluntarily to participate in the peer mediation process. Once the mediation is ready to begin, the supervising adult leaves the room and turns the process over to the mediator. During the session, the mediator may use a copy of the Peer Mediation Process Summary included in Appendix C to help him or her remember the steps. The adult remains in the area in case the mediator needs assistance. After 15 or 20 minutes, the supervisor can check with the mediator to be sure that everything is going along as expected.

When the mediation is completed and the disputants have signed an agreement (see the Peer Mediation Agreement in Appendix C), the supervising adult may reenter the room and look over the agreement to be sure everything is satisfactory.

PRESENT THE PROGRAM TO STUDENTS _____

The peer mediation program should be presented to students prior to the selection of the peer mediators. One recommended approach involves holding assemblies of no more than 100 students at a time. Such assemblies might be structured as follows.

1. Explain what peer mediation is, what its benefits are, and why peer mediators are important.

2. Role-play a peer mediation session. (Use a staff person or student familiar with the method as a mediator and students as disputants.)

3. Explain the ground rules and steps involved in peer mediation.

4. Present a second role-play.

5. Share the basic program procedures and project timeline.

6. Describe the process for selecting and training peer mediators.

7. Explain how students can apply to become peer mediators and hand out copies of the Peer Mediator Application (see Appendix C). Application forms should also be made available through teachers and support staff.

SELECT PEER MEDIATORS _____

Students will need no more than a week to return the completed application forms. After the application forms have been received, the selection process can begin. In a school of 800 to 1,000 students, it would be good to choose 25 to 30 students for training.

Obviously, the qualities a student brings to the peer mediation program are more significant than any training that could be offered. Select students who have good communication and thinking skills. They should be mature enough to keep information confidential and assertive enough to be able to enforce the rules in a peer mediation session. Consider students who are representative of a cross section of the school population. Do they represent the school community in terms of sex, race, ethnicity, culture, and neighborhood? Look for students who have the respect of their peers and some level of informal influence.

After peer mediators have been selected, the school principal should officially notify and congratulate them and obtain parents' permission for their participation. The Parent Notification and Permission Letter included in Appendix C may serve to inform both students and parents.

PROVIDE TRAINING FOR TRAINERS

To help train and supervise peer mediators, a number of staff or advisory committee members will need to go through more extensive training in conflict resolution and peer mediation procedures. Although the exact content of this training will vary with the time allowed and the particular needs of the staff, to cover the information in sufficient detail from 8 to 12 hours of training are required. The following list suggests the content of one possible staff training program.

1. A definition of conflict

2. Rationale for starting a peer mediation program

3. Overview of the basic theory of conflict

4. Discussion of the role of the peer mediator

5. Summary of steps in the mediation process

6. Mediation role-play example

7. Discussion of the program proposal, including the specific timeline and procedures

8. Discussion of selection and training of peer mediators

9. Overview of proposed promotional efforts

10. Role-playing practice

The program for staff can involve the use of the peer mediator training materials described in chapters 5 and 6, adapted as necessary.

KEEP RECORDS AND EVALUATE PROGRAM

With the assistance of the advisory committee, the program coordinators keep a log of completed peer mediation sessions and a file of all agreements. (Staple the request form to the agreement form and file them together.) Notification of a resolution can be given to each student's administrator, if desired.

Coordinators may also want to calculate totals to reflect such information as number of conflicts; type and place of conflicts; sex, grade, and race of disputants; who requested the mediation (student, faculty, administrator); and the amount of time the mediation took to complete. This record will help to evaluate the effectiveness of the program and confirm whether students are using the service. This information can be extracted from the Peer Mediation Request, the Peer Mediation Agreement, and school records. Information can be reported on a monthly or quarterly basis, as appropriate. The Peer Mediation Record-Keeping Form included in Appendix C can be adapted to any school's particular interests and needs.

In addition to compiling statistics, program coordinators may wish to conduct some follow-up interviews with former disputants and peer mediators. This will give a more in-depth idea of the quality of the program. During these follow-up interviews, disputants can be asked whether their resolution was fair and lasting. Mediators can help by reporting their peers' impressions of the program and by giving suggestions to improve the program.

The final part of the evaluation can be an assessment of whether the goals of the original proposal were met. Overall data can be generated to indicate the success with which peer mediation dealt with various types of conflicts. In addition, improvements in the areas of truancy, vandalism, suspensions, fighting, and the like can be noted. Although such improvements cannot be attributed solely to peer mediation, they can reflect a trend toward a more positive school climate, for which peer mediation may be in part responsible. (For a sample annual evaluation summary, see Appendix A.)

CHAPTER 4

Program Sponsorship and Promotion

Like many new ideas, peer mediation can be greeted with skepticism. Students may be reluctant to try the approach because it is new. Teachers may feel the program is just another intrusion into their already limited class time or, as veterans of various management approaches, may wonder how this program can succeed where others have failed. Effective resource development and sponsorship and a good promotional campaign will serve to enhance the status of peer mediators and the peer mediation program.

As the case example at the end of this chapter shows, efforts to find sponsorship for and promote a peer mediation program can be fun as well as informative. The success these endeavors can bring will be a valuable reinforcement for the staff and students who have worked so hard to develop the program—and for the parents and business and community sponsors who support them.

DEVELOPING RESOURCES AND OBTAINING SPONSORSHIP

If funding is needed, it makes sense first to consult school organizations like the PTA or student council about financial support for developing the project. Consider requesting general donations from individuals or from service organizations such as the Rotary Club, the Optimists Club, or the Urban League.

Because reducing conflicts between students adds to the reputation of the school and advances the interests of the community, local businesses may be especially interested in sponsoring a peer mediation program. Targeting businesses with interests related to families and children is a way to begin.

Individuals, organizations, or businesses are more likely to provide support when given an informational letter and brochure that identify your school and offer an outline of the program, its goals, and its benefits to the school and community. It can also be helpful to include a list of other individual, organizational, and business sponsors along with an estimate of the expenses you anticipate.

Some sponsors will prefer to know exactly how their money is being spent. If this is the case, consider requesting funds for specific items like T-shirts, food for a recognition event, pins, printing, and the like. Acknowledge contributions with thank-you letters and credit contributions in brochures, on T-shirts, in newsletters sent to parents, and so forth. Send supporters copies of any materials crediting them; many will also appreciate receiving updates on the project.

Make requests simple and transactions brief, follow up on agreements, and avoid any complications or disorganization that might make sponsors uneasy about contributing. Remember that even if the project lacks funds, a peer mediation program can still be established with the support of human resources.

PROMOTING THE PROGRAM

The basic goals of program promotion are as follows.

▲ To make students and staff aware of the importance of peer mediation as a peaceful alternative for resolving conflicts and to encourage them to participate in the program

▲ To establish an image that represents the program's goals and philosophy through the program's name, logo, and other promotional material

▲ To provide information about the program to the whole school community

▲ To communicate an idea of the types of conflicts that can be mediated

Whether the designers of the promotional campaign are students, teachers, parents, or members of a professional advertising agency volunteering their time, they need to understand what peer mediation is and what image is to be conveyed. In other words, promotion designers must know what they are selling. Discuss program goals with promoters and work together to develop a plan to accomplish these goals.

One way to begin to create an image is to examine the existing philosophy of the school and to assess the school climate. After this is done, ideas can be elicited for how peer mediation could enhance the quality of the school. These ideas provide the framework for establishing the image and influence the content of any promotional efforts.

A central factor in the development of an image is the type of conflicts the program will handle. For instance, if the program is ready to take on complex racial conflicts, then sobering statistics could be at the heart of the campaign. For those frequent, incidental conflicts brought about by rumor and gossip, it may be appropriate to use humor, outrageousness, or cartoons.

Identifying the program by a name and logo characterizing the peer mediation concept facilitates recognition and helps build the program's image. In choosing a name and logo, consider which students the program wishes to reach and what principles or ideas will be represented. Do the name and logo need to reflect current teen trends, or is it more important to consider the interests of sponsors or staff?

The program's name, its logo, and any "tag line" or slogan should appear in public prior to the opening of the peer mediation center. Ongoing promotional efforts should remind students and teachers that the peer mediation service is in operation. It is imperative to establish a positive identity for the program. If perceived in a negative way, the program will struggle to succeed. It is better to make statements about what peer mediation is than to be put in a defensive position by having to make statements about what it is not.

INVOLVING STUDENTS

Peer mediation is based on the belief that students can help students. Students know what motivates other students, and therefore it is prudent to involve them in the promotional campaign. If many students can be involved, it follows that ownership of the project will grow and public relations will be favorable.

Students can be involved at all levels of the promotional effort. They can distribute literature, act as program representatives, write public service announcements, set up a peer mediator recognition event, dispense pins and stickers, or demonstrate a peer mediation role-play. The search for a program name or logo could be developed by using a creative brainstorming process, with students working together to reach consensus. Possibilities are limited only by the degree of student motivation.

Students who design the promotion should demonstrate a facility with language, be strong "idea" people, and represent a range of varying points of view in the school population. Students from within the peer mediation program may volunteer to work on the promotion team; faculty may also make recommendations. The student council or the school newspaper could adopt the promotional effort as a special project. Many such combinations can work.

Give students deadlines and help them understand how to work within budget restrictions. Give guidelines that could help save money. Expect quality from students, help them evaluate the quality of their work, and they will produce a quality promotional campaign.

INVOLVING FACULTY

A peer mediation program establishes credibility if the faculty believe in it. When faculty are supportive and involved, they can become a peer mediation program's most valuable promotional asset.

It is important to consider faculty in all aspects of planning and promotion, especially if teaching time is involved. Discuss procedures at the mediation center and facilitate faculty members' understanding of their role in the mediation process. Ask faculty to inform program coordinators of any problems they observe.

If faculty will be asked to explain the mediation process to students, part of the promotional effort should include a packet of information about peer mediation. This packet could contain a simple handout explaining the program; relevant program forms; and any brochures, posters, or articles written about the program.

Faculty should be updated on the progress of the promotion and the program. Arrange a time and place for them to meet the new peer mediators, and acknowledge staff involvement and support for the program. Staff referrals show students the faculty believe the peer mediation process has merit; this in turn serves to validate the program from the students' perspective. Having the faculty endorse the program because they see it as a viable way for students to resolve their conflicts will ensure the program's success.

CASE EXAMPLE: COMMON GROUND

The rest of this chapter describes actual sponsorship and promotional efforts for Common Ground, the peer mediation program begun in

1988 at the Urbana, Illinois, Middle School. Although a strategy such as this one this will not be appropriate for every school, it does illustrate how resources were combined to shape the plan. Many of the techniques used may be adapted in other schools.

The Urbana program was supported by school funds and donations from a corporate sponsor, a local food distribution company. Corporate sponsorship was obtained by a retired teacher who remains active as a community liaison between the school and local businesses. After she discovered that this company had an employee management mediation center, she approached the personnel director with the school's plan. Her outreach resulted in funding for printing of all of the peer mediation literature; T-shirts for peer mediators, staff trainers, and advisory committee members; and catering for a recognition luncheon. Miscellaneous funds from various school clubs and organizations paid for pins and art supplies.

Three students in a graphic design class were responsible for developing promotional materials. The students were given this special assignment because they were interested and good "idea" people. A parent who is a professional graphic designer and illustrator in the community volunteered to assist them.

After poring over dozens of graphic design and art magazines, the students came up with sketches for logos, color schemes, and suggestions for names and tag lines. According to them, the development of the main concept was the hardest part of the whole campaign, and they worked intensely for 2 weeks before they came up with any designs that they felt were satisfactory. Their plan was designed to convey the images of gentle humor and sincerity.

The peer mediators, program coordinators, and staff involved in the project voted on their favorite options. Once decisions were made, the design students created mock-ups of a brochure for adults, a brochure for students, posters, flyers, T-shirts, pins, and invitations to a recognition luncheon. (The text of the brochures for adults and students is reproduced in Figures 2 and 3, respectively. A sample poster is presented in Figure 4.) The program name (Common Ground), logo, and tag line ("students helping students") were prepared for presentation to the school administration and the program's corporate sponsor.

Throughout the week prior to the grand opening, morning announcements, written and read by peer mediators on the public address system, helped explain the mediation concept and added to the excitement. A teacher involved in the program volunteered along with other teachers who were supporters of the project to organize a luncheon to recognize the peer mediators. She made arrangements with the catering department of a local grocery store and mailed invitations to mediators and parents, sponsors, administrators, school board members, the school district superintendent, and special guests. Decorations were set up by the peer mediators.

The recognition luncheon took place the day before the grand opening. The luncheon was well attended, and the principal welcomed guests and publicly thanked the school and community sponsors and organizers. After lunch, mediation demonstrations were given by peer mediators, and the school social worker explained the process to parents and sponsors. The peer mediators received special certificates and official T-shirts and were honored by parents, teachers, friends, and members of the business community.

After the luncheon, selected peer mediators were interviewed by local media reporters. Later that day, after all the other students were gone, the mediators covered the school with flyers and posters that would signal the opening of the Common Ground mediation center. Flyers were posted on most student lockers, and posters were displayed throughout the cafeteria and even in the bathroom stalls. Teachers displayed posters in their classrooms depicting the mediation center's logo and explaining referral procedures.

The morning of the grand opening, students entered the school to find posters and flyers everywhere. Announcements over the public address system noted the official opening of the mediation center. All peer mediators and teachers who were part of the program wore their T-shirts. During first hour, teachers distributed brochures and explained the mediation process, discussed procedures for referrals, and answered questions. At lunch, students were given the chance to meet their grade-level peer mediators at tables set up near the lunch lines. The mediators handed out pins that read "Start Talking—Common Ground Mediation."

The next day after school, the faculty assembled in the library for coffee, after which the principal introduced the peer mediators. The mediators received enthusiastic applause and thanks from teachers and support staff. During that same week, brochures were mailed to all parents and news releases were sent to the local media. Several requests for mediation were made within the first few days of the center's operation. These requests continued throughout the school year.

When the first group of peer mediators filled out evaluations at the end of the year, they were asked if they had it to do over again whether they would choose to participate. They unanimously answered yes. The campaign had succeeded in establishing an effective alternative for resolving conflicts.

Figure 2 Sample Staff and Community Brochure

Conflicts Are Part of Everyday Life

At Urbana Middle School students have a positive way to settle conflicts called *mediation*. Common Ground is the name of the in-school mediation center where students help students mediate their own disputes.

Student Conflicts Are Common

At Urbana Middle School, the most typical conflicts between students are:

- ▲ "He said/she said" rumors
- ▲ Name-calling
- ▲ Friendships gone amiss
- ▲ Threats

Student conflicts that are not resolved may end up with loss of friends, verbal attacks, and disruptive behaviors that can make learning more difficult.

Mediation: A Tool to Resolve Conflicts

Mediation has been used in many settings as a positive and structured approach to settle disputes. It is a voluntary and cooperative process where two parties who are having a conflict communicate with each other and look for agreement. It is a problem-solving approach where no one loses.

Mediation at Urbana Middle School is used to resolve student disputes because it empowers students to:

- ▲ Communicate more effectively across age and cultural differences
- ▲ Develop empathy and the skills of listening, oral expression, and critical thinking
- ▲ Address problems of hostility, aggression, and absenteeism in a peaceful way

A select number of students are trained to act as mediators. The student mediators facilitate the process when a request is made. In this way, students are given an opportunity to solve their own problems without an adult's doing it for them.

How the Center Was Established

Steps were undertaken during the fall to establish the center. Highlights of this process were:

Staff orientation: Staff were given an overview of the mediation process and the purpose of the student mediation center. Interested staff were asked to volunteer for the advisory committee.

Student assemblies: Grade level assemblies were held to explain mediation and the center. At this time any students who were interested in becoming mediators applied.

Mediator selection: A diverse group of students were selected from those who applied. Ten students from each grade level were chosen by the advisory committee.

Training of mediators: The selected students were given 15–20 hours of training in the skill of conflict resolution.

Procedures for Mediation

The advisory committee established guidelines for the center:

- ▲ Any student can request mediation.
- ▲ Students can be referred to mediation by faculty, administrators, or parents.
- ▲ All parties must agree voluntarily to the process.
- ▲ All parties involved agree to confidentiality.
- ▲ Disputants come up with their own solutions and an agreement is signed.

Ongoing Training and Evaluation

Records are kept and the advisory committee will assess the effectiveness of the center. Ongoing training and support are given to the student mediators.

Steps in the Mediation Process

STEP 1: Open the session

- ▲ Make introductions.
- ▲ State the ground rules.

STEP 2: Gather information

- ▲ Ask each person to tell what happened.
- ▲ Ask each person whether he or she wants to add anything.

STEP 3: Focus on common interests

- ▲ Determine and summarize shared interests.

STEP 4: Create options

- ▲ Brainstrorm solutions and ask disputants what can be done to resolve the problem.

STEP 5: Evaluate options and choose a solution

- ▲ Ask each person what could be done to resolve the problem.

STEP 6: Write the agreement and close

- ▲ Write up the agreement and have disputants sign it.
- ▲ Shake hands.

Benefits

Mediation promotes a positive school environment in which students learn a peaceful way to resolve conflicts. This process teaches mutual respect through clear and direct communication. This life skill can be applied to the family, neighborhood, and community.

Students are empowered with a strategy to deal successfully with everyday problems, ultimately resulting in enhanced self-esteem and positive changes in behavior.

Figure 3 Sample Student Brochure

Having a conflict?

- ▲ Has someone made fun of you or teased you?
- ▲ Did someone say, "Just wait and I'll get you after school?"
- ▲ Did "he say" that "she said" that "you said" . . . and a rumor is going around the school?

What is mediation?

Mediation is a chance for you to sit face to face and talk, uninterrupted, so each side of the dispute is heard. After the problem is defined, solutions are created and then evaluated. When an agreement is reached, it is written and signed.

What is a student mediator?

A student mediator is one of your peers who has been trained to conduct the mediation meeting. The student mediator makes sure the mediation session is helpful and fair. Your fellow students were selected to help you resolve differences because they might better understand your point of view.

Are there any rules in mediation?

To make the process work, there are a few simple rules.

1. Mediation is a process that both students choose.
2. Everything said during a mediation is kept confidential. What is said in the room stays in the room.
3. In mediation, students take turns talking and no one can interrupt.
4. The student mediator does not take sides.

If I have a conflict, how do I go about getting it mediated?

It is very easy to request a mediation. Just pick up a mediation request form from a counselor or social worker. Take 2 minutes to fill it out and return it to any counselor or social worker. Within a day you will receive notification of the time and place of mediation. Mediations will be scheduled when the least amount of class time is missed.

Why should I try mediation?

There are many reasons why mediation will be helpful to you. Here are a few.

1. Conflicts that do not get resolved often end in fights, which could result in suspension.
2. Conflicts that do not get resolved often result in hurt feelings, which could cause you to lose friends.
3. You will learn to choose a peaceful, responsible way to solve your own problems without an adult's doing it for you.
4. Mediation will help you develop mutual respect and clear communication.
5. Mediation will make school a more positive place to learn and grow.

If you answered yes to any of these questions, check out Common Ground, Urbana Middle School's student mediation center.

Figure 4 Sample Poster

CHAPTER 5

Peer Mediator Training: Core Activities

This chapter presents detailed instructions for conducting a sequence of 14 core training activities to orient peer mediators to the program and help them master the basic steps in the mediation process. This training will give students the skills they need to conduct most of the peer mediations that will be requested. Chapter 6 gives step-by-step instructions for a number of activities for ongoing peer mediator training and support.

TRAINING ACTIVITIES AND AGENDA

The training activities range in length from 10 to 90 minutes. In the activities, instructions are given to read aloud corresponding segments of the Student Manual. Trainers should feel free to modify this suggestion according to their own circumstances. Student volunteers may be invited to read the selections aloud, or study of these selections might be undertaken as a cooperative learning activity. For ease in teaching, readings and worksheets from the Student Manual have been reproduced here as shaded portions.

The equivalent of 2 days of training will be needed to conduct all of the core training activities. Training may be accomplished in either full- or half-day sessions. A sample agenda, presented in Figure 5, outlines a workshop to conduct the core training activities in 2 consecutive days. The times noted for each activity are a general guideline—any given group may need more or less time than suggested.

STAFFING

The entire workshop can be delivered by one or two trainers—the program coordinators or other adults with communication/mediation experience. Alternatively, different parts of the workshop may be delivered by different members of the program's advisory committee.

In addition to the main trainers, advisory committee members or other members of the school staff will need to participate and help with the activities. A ratio of one adult to three or four students is best. Training can be successful with anywhere from 15 to 40 peer mediators; an ideal size for the training workshop would be 30 peer mediators and 10 teachers or other staff members.

Figure 5 Sample 2-Day Agenda: Core Training

DAY 1	**Morning**
8:30– 9:00	Boundary Breakers
9:00– 9:10	Activity 1: Welcome and Overview of Training
9:10– 9:30	Activity 2: Introduction to Peer Mediation
9:30– 10:30	Activity 3: Understanding Conflict
10:30– 10:45	*Break*
10:45– 11:15	Activity 4: Qualities and Role of the Peer Mediator
11:15– 12:15	Activity 5: Communication Skills
12:15– 1:00	*Lunch*

	Afternoon
1:00– 1:15	Activity 6: Overview of the Peer Mediation Process
1:15– 1:25	Activity 7: Preparing for Peer Mediation
1:25– 1:40	Activity 8: Open the Session (Step 1)
1:40– 2:20	Activity 9: Gather Information (Step 2)
2:20– 2:30	*Break*
2:30– 3:00	Activity 10—Part I: Focus on Common Interests (Step 3)
3:00– 3:15	Closure Activities

DAY 2	**Morning**
8:30– 9:00	Boundary Breakers
9:00– 10:00	Activity 10—Part II: Review and Role-Playing of Steps 1 through 3
10:00– 10:30	Activity 11: Create Options (Step 4)
10:30– 10:45	*Break*
10:45– 11:15	Activity 12: Evaluate Options and Choose a Solution (Step 5)
11:15– 11:45	Activity 13—Part I: Write the Agreement and Close (Step 6)
11:45– 12:30	*Lunch*

	Afternoon
12:30– 12:45	Boundary Breakers
12:45– 1:45	Activity 13—Part II: Review and Role-Playing of Steps 1 through 6
1:45– 2:00	*Break*
2:00– 2:30	Activity 14: Supporting Yourself and Others
2:30– 3:00	Closure Activities

TRAINING ENVIRONMENT

The best environment for the training workshop is a large room with movable chairs and a number of small round tables. The chairs and tables should be arranged in a semicircle so the participants can make eye contact with the trainers and one another. If possible, try to find a location for the training off school grounds. Leaving school will make the experience special and exciting.

TRAINING MATERIALS

Materials needed for training include the following items.

1. A Student Manual for each participant
2. Photocopies of selected forms, as specified in each training activity
3. Chalkboard or flip chart
4. Newsprint and markers
5. Pens or pencils
6. Name tags
7. Masking tape

TIPS FOR SUCCESSFUL TRAINING

To conduct training most effectively, trainers will need to promote a climate that encourages participants to take risks, share, and become actively involved. The atmosphere must be cooperative and supportive; all students must be directly involved in the activities and practice the skills. Some specific suggestions to promote learning are as follows.

1. Post the training agenda as well as your expectations for behavior and participation.
2. Use boundary breakers and closure activities like those described in Appendix D at the beginning and end of each training segment.
3. Be sure all trainers participate in activities and share. Trainers' thoughts and feelings are important, too.
4. Model good communication skills by actively listening, summarizing, and clarifying student responses.
5. Use a self-evaluation process instead of having an adult judge the quality of students' work.
6. Help students who resist or feel uncomfortable with a topic or exercise to express themselves by talking about someone they may know instead of themselves.
7. Be enthusiastic and show acceptance by smiling and approving. Your positive energy will rub off.

1   **Welcome and Overview of Training**

PURPOSE   Students will receive an official welcome to peer mediator training and a brief overview of what training will involve.

TIME   10 minutes

MATERIALS   Student Manual (Reading for Activity 1)

PROCEDURE

1. Welcome students to peer mediation training and ask them to open their manuals to the reading for Activity 1. Read aloud.

> Congratulations on being selected a peer mediator.
>
> You were selected because—
>
> ▲ Your teachers felt you have the *qualities* necessary to be a skilled mediator.
>
> ▲ You have *good judgment* and the *respect* of your peers. You are probably a person other students can talk to and *trust*.
>
> ▲ You represent one of the various groups that make up the school. As you know, every school has a variety of people, personalities, cultures, and ethnic groups. We want you to speak from your *personal experience* and for the peers you represent.
>
> In this training workshop, we want to build on your positive qualities and abilities. We will teach you how to help students who are in conflict work together to solve their own problems. This process of conflict resolution is called *peer mediation*.
>
> Specifically, you will learn—
>
> ▲ The causes and results of conflict
>
> ▲ The role of the mediator
>
> ▲ Communication skills
>
> ▲ Steps in the mediation process
>
> The workshop is experiential, which means you will learn by doing. Everyone will have a chance to share ideas and experiences about conflict and to practice peer mediation situations. This training is an opportunity to increase your knowledge of conflict, learn the skills of conflict resolution, and have fun.

2. Before moving on, give students a chance to ask any questions they might have.

PURPOSE Students will become familiar with the goals of peer mediation, the role of the peer mediator, and assumptions underlying the approach.

TIME 20 minutes

MATERIALS Student Manual (Reading for Activity 2)

PROCEDURE

1. Explain that peer mediation seeks to give responsibility, control, and power to the people who can best solve student problems—the students themselves. Have them refer to the reading for Activity 2 in their manuals. Read aloud the following section, then briefly discuss.

PEER MEDIATION: DEFINITION AND GOALS

Mediation is an approach to resolve conflict in which the **disputants**, or the people who disagree, have the chance to sit face to face and talk uninterrupted so each side of the dispute is heard. After the problem is defined, solutions are created and then evaluated. When an agreement is reached, it is written and signed.

The goals of peer mediation are as follows.

▲ For disputants to understand and respect different views

▲ To open and improve communication

▲ To develop cooperation in solving a common problem

▲ To reach agreements that address the interests of both sides

When one person wins and another loses in a dispute, we say it is a **win/lose situation**. Sometimes both people can lose in a conflict situation, as is the case when someone works so hard to hurt the other person that he or she also gets hurt. We call this a **lose/lose situation**. Peer mediation is a **win/win approach** to conflict: Both people are winners, and no one loses.

2. Continue in the reading with the following description of the role of the peer mediator. Briefly discuss and answer any questions.

ROLE OF THE PEER MEDIATOR

A trained peer mediator is a neutral third person who leads the mediation process. The mediator helps the disputants communicate and keeps all information *confidential.* This means not discussing the disputants' problem with other students in the school. Peer mediators—

▲ Are the peacemakers for the school

▲ Listen to and respect all points of view

▲ Understand their own conflicts and how to handle them

▲ Know how to help other students resolve their conflicts.

3. Continue in the reading with the discussion of assumptions underlying the peer mediation approach.

ASSUMPTIONS OF PEER MEDIATION

It takes cooperation and understanding to resolve conflicts. Peer mediation is based on the belief that, in order to resolve conflicts, people must be willing to do the following.

▲ Stay calm and control their anger

▲ Focus on the problem and not blame the other person

▲ Honestly state their wants and feelings

▲ Understand and respect the other person's point of view

▲ Cooperate and create solutions that meet the needs of everyone involved

4. Briefly discuss the assumptions underlying peer mediation and address any questions students might have. Reiterate the point that in a successful peer mediation, everyone wins and no one loses.

3   **Understanding Conflict**

PURPOSE   Students will learn that conflict is a potentially positive force, understand the source of conflict, and learn the possible responses to conflict. In addition, they will develop some ideas about what happens when a conflict is resolved and when it is not.

TIME   60 minutes

MATERIALS   Student Manual (Reading for Activity 3)
Newsprint
Markers

PROCEDURE

1. Begin by explaining that the upcoming activities will increase students' understanding of conflict.

2. Ask students to refer to the Defining Conflict worksheet in the reading for Activity 3. Read the word *conflict* and ask students to write down the first word or phrase that comes to mind. Read the word *conflict* four more times, each time asking students to write down another word or phrase.

Worksheet: *Defining Conflict*

PART I
Conflict _____
Conflict _____
Conflict _____
Conflict _____
Conflict _____
PART II
Conflict _____
Conflict _____
Conflict _____
Conflict _____
Conflict _____

---

3. Invite students to share some of their responses. Typical responses will include *fight, argument, war, disagreement, hassle, controversy, struggle,* and *battle.*

4. Divide into groups of four or five and give each group markers and a large sheet of newsprint. Encourage each group to compile a list of conflicts that they have had or know about. Give each group one of the following categories: family, friends, teachers, community, or world.

5. After 5 minutes, have each group share their lists. Point out how these and other conflicts are examples of challenges that we can learn from and that they test our communication and problem-solving skills. Post the lists so they can be referred to as examples throughout training.

6. Refer students to the statements about conflict in their manuals. Read aloud, then discuss.

STATEMENTS ABOUT CONFLICT

People live, work, and play together, and it is important for them to get along. To do so, people must understand the following ideas about conflict.

- ▲ Conflict is a natural part of everyday life.
- ▲ Conflict can be handled in positive or negative ways.
- ▲ Conflict can have either creative or destructive results.
- ▲ Conflict can be a positive force for personal growth and social change.

7. Direct students once more to the Defining Conflict worksheet. Repeat the word *conflict* again, asking students to write down five additional words or phrases that suggest positive results of conflict.

8. Invite students to share their new responses and explain how these new responses were different from before. Summarize by repeating the point that, even though conflicts can be painful, they are opportunities to grow.

9. Read aloud the following section from the manual.

BASIC NEEDS

Understanding how to resolve a conflict begins with identifying the source of the conflict. Most every dispute between people involves the attempt to meet certain basic needs for belonging, power, freedom, or fun.

- ▲ *Belonging:* Loving, sharing, and cooperating with others
- ▲ *Power:* Achieving, accomplishing, and being recognized and respected
- ▲ *Freedom:* Making choices in our lives
- ▲ *Fun:* Laughing and playing

We might think that people or situations cause us to act a certain way, but this belief is not true. We act the way we do because we are trying to meet our basic needs. For instance, suppose you are upset because your friend is going to a party and you were not invited. You might get into a conflict with the friend because you are not getting your need for *belonging* met. Or suppose you are in conflict with a parent about the chores you must do around the house. This conflict might be the result of your need to have the *freedom* to make your own choices about how to spend your time.

10. Point out that being aware of how we get our basic needs met helps us to identify unmet needs as a source of conflict. Refer students to the Meeting Basic Needs worksheet in the reading and give them 5 minutes to complete it.

Worksheet: Meeting Basic Needs

Directions: Write down the things you do to get your needs met in each of the
following areas.

1. ***Belonging:*** Loving, sharing, and cooperating with others
2. ***Power:*** Achieving, accomplishing, and being recognized and respected
3. ***Freedom:*** Making choices in our lives
4. ***Fun:*** Laughing and playing

11. Divide students into groups of four or five. Ask them to share and compare the ways they meet
their needs in the four basic areas. Use the following questions to help process this part of the
activity.

▲ What were some of the differences in your group?

▲ Do you ever change what you choose to do to get your needs met?

▲ What would cause you to make such a change?

12. Continue with the reading, then discuss.

LIMITED RESOURCES AND DIFFERENT VALUES

Often limited resources or different values appear to be the underlying cause of
conflicts.

Conflicts that involve ***limited resources*** can be about a lack of time, money, or
property. For instance, two classmates are having a conflict over property when they
are arguing about who will get to use a certain book they both want for a report.

When people in conflict talk about honesty, equal rights, or fairness, the conflict is
probably about ***different values***. People have different convictions, priorities, and
principles, and these differences can mean conflict. For instance, a student who values
honesty in her friends will probably be very upset and angry if a friend lies to her.
Conflicts involving values tend to be difficult to resolve because when people's values
are different, they often perceive the dispute as a personal attack. Resolving a values
conflict does not mean the disputants must change or align their values. Often a
mutual acknowledgment that each person views the situation differently is the first
step toward resolution.

Unmet needs are at the heart of conflicts over limited resources and different values.
We want certain resources (time, money, property) or hold certain values (honesty,
fairness, equality) because they satisfy basic needs. Resources and values are ***wants***.
We choose wants to satisfy our needs.

So, the two classmates fighting over the book they both want for a report are really
attempting to get their ***power*** needs met. If they fail the class or do not write a quality
report, they will not be accomplishing or achieving, and they may not be recognized or

respected by themselves or others. Likewise, the student who is angry because her friend lied to her is attempting to get her *belonging* need met. She finds it difficult to share and cooperate with someone who is not honest.

13. Next ask students to turn to the Understanding the Source of Conflict worksheet in the manual. Give them about 5 minutes to complete the worksheet.

Worksheet: Understanding the Source of Conflict

Directions: Describe a recent conflict you had at school.

1. Who was involved?
2. How did you feel?
3. What did the other person want?
4. What did you want?
5. Were limited resources or different values involved in the conflict? If so, how?
6. What do you think the unmet basic need or needs were behind the conflict? (Remember, these needs could be for belonging, power, freedom, or fun.)

14. Ask students to share some of their conflicts. Invite group feedback about the probable unmet needs underlying each conflict.

15. Next refer students to the discussion in the manual on responses to conflict. Read aloud, then briefly discuss.

RESPONSES TO CONFLICT

People can choose one of three ways of responding to conflict: avoidance, confrontation, or communication.

Avoidance

People avoid conflict by withdrawing from the situation, ignoring the problem, or denying their feelings. Avoiding the conflict may help in the short run—for instance, it might help someone keep from losing his temper. However, avoidance usually makes a person doubt himself or feel anxious about the future. In addition, because the conflict is never brought up, it can never be resolved. As a result, the person's basic needs are never met.

Confrontation

Confrontation in response to conflict means a person expresses anger, verbal or physical threats, or aggression. It may also mean the person resorts to bribery or to punishments like withholding money, favors, or affection. These actions show a win/lose attitude toward conflict. The attitude that one person must win and the other person must lose in a conflict prevents cooperation and keeps people from reaching a mutually satisfying solution.

Communication

Communication in response to conflict means to participate in a common understanding, not necessarily to agree. In order for people to cooperate, they must first communicate. People in conflict who seek first to understand the other person's side, then be understood, produce win/win resolutions. In other words, both people get their needs met, and no one loses.

16. Ask students to complete the Identifying Responses to Conflict worksheet in the reading, then circle their three most common responses to conflict. After students have finished, read each response aloud and ask for thumbs up if they feel the response is helpful and thumbs down if they feel it is not.

Worksheet: Identifying Responses to Conflict

Directions: Check whether you think these responses are examples of avoidance, confrontation, or communication. Then circle the numbers of the three responses you most commonly use when in conflict.

1. Ignore the situation *(avoidance)*
2. Threaten the other person *(confrontation)*
3. Fight it out *(confrontation)*
4. Just give in—it doesn't really matter *(avoidance)*
5. Try to discover new possibilities *(communication)*
6. Complain until I get my way *(confrontation)*
7. Admit differences *(communication)*
8. Admit I am wrong, even if I don't think so *(avoidance)*
9. Change the subject *(avoidance)*
10. Try to understand the other person's point of view *(communication)*

17. To review concepts taught so far, ask students to refer to the Conflict Diagram in the reading (see Figure 6) and encourage them to say what they think is the most important thing they have learned about conflict.

18. Next have students divide into small groups and choose a reporter for each group. Give each group a sheet of newsprint and a marker. Ask half of the groups to make a list of what might happen if a conflict is resolved. Ask the other half to make a list of what might happen if a conflict is not resolved. After about 10 minutes, ask each reporter to share responses. Some possible outcomes if conflicts remain unresolved are as follows.

▲ Threats and blame continue.

▲ Feelings are hurt, relationships are damaged.

▲ Self-interest results, positions harden.

▲ Emotions increase, tempers get out of hand.

- ▲ Sides are drawn, other people get involved.
- ▲ People do not get what they want and need.
- ▲ Violence can result.

Here are some possible outcomes if people work together for agreement.

- ▲ Better ideas are produced to solve the problem.
- ▲ Relationships and communication are improved.
- ▲ Views are clarified, problems are dealt with.
- ▲ People listen to and respect each other.
- ▲ There is cooperation.
- ▲ People get what they want and need.
- ▲ Fairness and peace are achieved.

Figure 6 Conflict Diagram

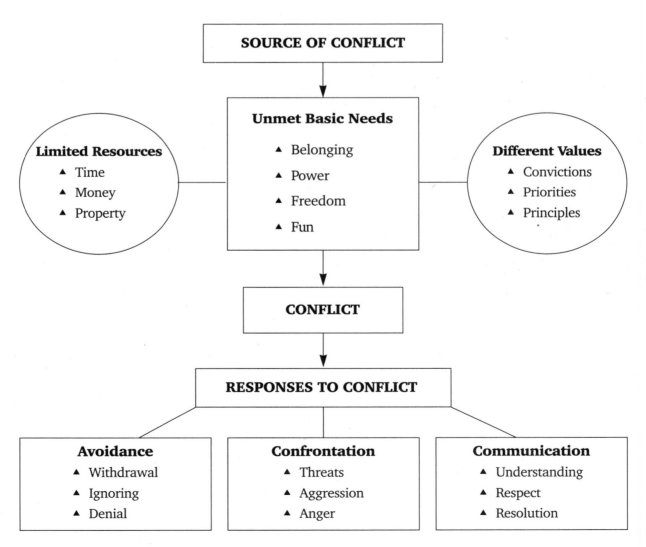

4   Qualities and Role of the Peer Mediator

PURPOSE   Students will develop an awareness of the qualities of an effective peer mediator and an understanding of their role in the peer mediation process.

TIME   30 minutes

MATERIALS   Student Manual (Reading for Activity 4)
Yardstick
A pair of cowboy boots and a pair of ballet slippers
A length of rope, 4 to 6 feet long

PROCEDURE

1. Briefly state the purpose of the activity and explain that students were selected to be mediators based on their personal qualities.

2. Ask students to turn to the Statements About Me worksheet in the reading for Activity 4. Explain that this worksheet is designed to help students understand their own personal qualities and therefore become better peer mediators. Allow students a few minutes to complete the statements.

Worksheet: Statements About Me

Directions: Complete the statements by writing the first response that comes to mind.

1. My friends say that I . . .
2. I sometimes wish . . .
3. I feel best when . . .
4. One way I relax is . . .
5. I get frustrated with . . .
6. In school I . . .
7. I feel disappointed when . . .
8. I am good at . . .
9. My parents expect . . .
10. Two words that describe me are . . .
11. When I get angry I . . .
12. When I trust someone I . . .
13. I think a friend is . . .
14. I know prejudice can . . .
15. I will be an effective peer mediator because . . .

3. Have the students divide into groups of three to discuss their statements.

4. Reassemble as a larger group to discuss the following questions.

▲ What did your group have in common?

▲ What differences did you discover?

▲ Were you surprised about anything?

▲ What qualities do you think will make you an effective peer mediator?

5. Have students turn to the beginning of the reading. Present and discuss the five characteristics of the peer mediator, one at a time. Follow each explanation with a demonstration, as described.

1. The peer mediator remains **unbiased**.

   A mediator is neutral and objective, a person who does not take sides.

Demonstrate by balancing the yardstick on your forefinger. Say, "The mediator is responsible for maintaining balance and, to be fair, must not be influenced by the emotions and stories of either side. If the mediator moves to one side or the other, the balance is lost and the mediation process will not work." Show how losing the balance point will make the yardstick fall.

2. The peer mediator is an **empathic listener**.

   A mediator is skilled at listening with the intent to understand what each disputant thinks and feels.

Demonstrate by placing the cowboy boots and the ballet slippers on the floor and by standing first behind one pair of shoes and then behind the other while stating, "The mediator must listen with empathy to be able to understand what it's like to stand in each disputant's shoes."

3. The peer mediator is **respectful**.

   A mediator is able to treat both parties with respect and understanding, and without prejudice.

Demonstrate by saying, "The essence of being respectful is not that you agree with someone; it is that you understand the person's emotions and beliefs. You might not like the way the person's shoes fit—you may know you would never agree to dance in a pair of cowboy boots or ride a horse in ballet slippers—but as a mediator you do need to show disputants you understand the shoes they wear are important to them and to their situation."

To illustrate that the mediator must not have prejudices, stand by the cowboy boots and say, "Tell me some of your assumptions about someone who would wear these boots." Allow the students a minute or so to share their ideas. Then repeat, using the ballet slippers.

After the students share their ideas, tell them the cowboy boots belong to a grandmother and the ballet slippers belong to a professional football player. Explain that the key to being respectful is knowing that all people are different and that you run the risk of blocking communication, trust, and cooperation if you stereotype them.

Demonstrate by taking the length of rope and asking for two volunteers. Have the two volunteers tug on opposite ends of the rope while you hold the rope in the middle. (You will be pulled first one way, then the other.) Next ask the two students to hold the ends of the rope while they sit on the floor. Encourage them to figure out a way to raise themselves to a standing position by pulling on the rope. (It will be necessary for them to work together to do this.)

Ask for six to eight volunteers to help you in a trust exercise: Instruct participants to form a line. Each person in the line places his or her hands on the shoulders of the person in front. All but the last person in the line close their eyes. The last person in the line gives directions to the first person in the line for traveling around the room without running into furniture or other people. Give all of the students a chance to participate, then ask them how they felt about the experience. Did the people with their eyes closed trust the people who were helping them? What do they think this experience has to do with maintaining confidentiality in a peer mediation session?

6. Conclude by stating that the main role of the peer mediator is to build trust and cooperation, which in turn make mutual problem solving possible.

PURPOSE   Students will learn what communication is and become familiar with the basic communication skills of active listening, summarizing, and clarifying.

TIME   60 minutes

MATERIALS   Student Manual (Reading for Activity 5)
Six labels, prepared before the activity begins with the following phrases: *interrupt me, give me advice, make fun of me, criticize me, judge me,* and *tell me your problems*

PROCEDURE

1. To begin, indicate the purpose and importance of communication as the basis for problem solving. Point out that conflict often arises because of problems in communication.

2. Ask for six volunteers. Place six chairs or desks in a circle. Place a prepared label on each student's forehead without letting that person read it.

3. Instruct students to respond to one another according to the phrases on their labels. Give them 3 or 4 minutes to discuss and plan the next school dance (cost, place, music, theme, decorations, and clean-up).

4. After the time is up, process the exercise by asking the participating students how they thought they had been labeled and how they felt when people communicated and interacted with them based on their respective labels. Emphasize the point that labeling keeps people from communicating clearly.

5. Refer students to the reading for Activity 5 in their manuals. Read aloud, then discuss briefly.

> **Communication** occurs when a listener hears and understands a speaker's essential thoughts, acts, and feelings. Many conflicts continue because of poor communication between people. In order to communicate, the peer mediator uses the following specific communication skills: active listening, summarizing, and clarifying.
>
> **ACTIVE LISTENING**
>
> **Active listening** means using **nonverbal behaviors** to show you hear and understand. These nonverbal behaviors include tone of voice, eye contact, facial expressions, posture, and gestures. If you are leaning forward, smiling, nodding your head, and ignoring outside distractions, you are actively listening.

6. To practice active listening, have each student find a partner and face that person: One person talks while the other listens. The speaker should talk uninterrupted for 1 minute about the perfect Saturday night. During this time, the listener should demonstrate active listening skills. After the minute is up, the two partners switch roles. To process the exercise, discuss the following questions.

▲ *(To the listener)* Was it difficult to listen without interrupting? Why or why not?

▲ *(To the speaker)* What active listening skills did the listener use to help keep you talking?

7. Continue with the reading, then discuss.

SUMMARIZING

Summarizing means you do two things. First, you ***restate facts*** by repeating the most important points, organizing interests, and discarding extra information. Second, you ***reflect feelings*** about the conflict. It is very important when summarizing to recognize feelings in the situation as well as facts.

---

8. To practice summarizing facts and feelings, have the students again face their partners: One person talks uninterrupted for 1 minute about a recent conflict while the listener demonstrates active listening skills. After the minute is up, the listener summarizes facts and reflects feelings. The partners then switch roles. Process the exercise by discussing the following questions.

▲ *(To the listener)* Was it difficult to summarize both facts and feelings accurately? Why or why not?

▲ *(To the speaker)* Did the listener accurately summarize the information? How did the listener show understanding of your feelings?

9. Continue with the reading, then discuss.

CLARIFYING

Clarifying means using ***open-ended questions or statements*** to get additional information and to make sure you understand. Some examples of open-ended questions include—

▲ How did you feel about that? (question)

▲ Tell me what happened next in the situation. (statement)

▲ What do you think is keeping you from reaching an agreement about this problem? (question)

Open-ended questions can be answered in many different ways and help keep people talking. Closed questions can only be answered yes or no, and closed statements do not really require any response at all. Closed questions and statements such as the following tend to discourage people from further discussion.

▲ Did you feel angry when that happened? (yes-or-no question)

▲ You've been fighting for a long time. (no response needed)

▲ Do you think you can reach an agreement about this problem? (yes-or-no question)

10. To practice clarifying, have students face their partners again: One person talks on the topic of a recent conflict. The other actively listens, summarizes, and clarifies, continuing this cycle until the conflict is clearly defined and understood. Then the partners switch roles. To process the activity, discuss the following questions.

   ▲ *(To the listener)* What was the most difficult thing about clarifying?

   ▲ *(To the speaker)* Did the listener summarize after each statement and use open-ended questions or statements to get additional information? Do you think the listener clearly understood the conflict?

11. Continue with the reading, then discuss.

COMMUNICATION PITFALLS

In addition to using closed questions or statements, here are some sure-fire ways a peer mediator can shut down communication.

▲ Interrupt	▲ Laugh or ridicule
▲ Offer advice	▲ Criticize
▲ Judge	▲ Bring up your own experience

Be sure to avoid these common pitfalls!

12. Ask students to refer to the Communication Skills Diagram in the reading (see Figure 7). Discuss any questions they may have about the three communication skills.

Figure 7 Communication Skills Diagram

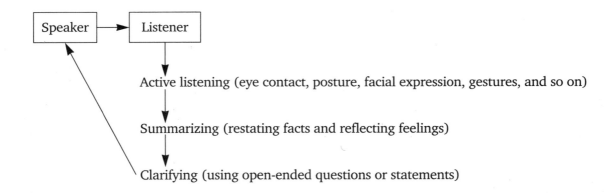

13. Ask students to fill out the Are You an Effective Communicator worksheet as a final review. When they are finished, invite them to comment briefly on how they feel they might improve their communication skills.

Worksheet: Are You an Effective Communicator?

Directions: Use this checklist to evaluate your communication skills.

1. Do you make eye contact?
2. Do you watch the person's body posture and facial expressions?
3. Do you empathize and try to understand feelings, thoughts, and actions?
4. Do you keep from interrupting and let the person finish, even though you already know what the person means?
5. Do you ask questions to clarify information?
6. Do you smile and nod your head to show interest?
7. Do you listen, even if you do not like the person who is talking or what the person is saying?
8. Do you ignore outside distractions?
9. Do you listen for and remember important points?
10. Do you keep from judging what was said—do you remain neutral?

6   Overview of the Peer Mediation Process

PURPOSE   Students will receive a brief overview of the six steps in the mediation process and will see the steps demonstrated.

TIME   15 minutes

MATERIALS   Student Manual (Reading for Activity 6)

PROCEDURE

1. State the purpose of the activity, then have the students refer to the list of steps in peer mediation in the reading for Activity 6 in their manuals. Briefly describe the peer mediation process.

STEPS IN PEER MEDIATION

STEP 1   Open the session

STEP 2   Gather information

STEP 3   Focus on common interests

STEP 4   Create options

STEP 5   Evaluate options and choose a solution

STEP 6   Write the agreement and close

---

2. With your co-trainers, give a demonstration of the case example presented in the manual.

CASE EXAMPLE

The following case example shows how a peer mediator used the six steps to help two students reach an agreement. In this situation, Michael and Sondra were referred to the mediation center by the school principal, Mr. Thomas.

STEP 1: *Open the session*

Mediator: Hello, my name is_____ and I am the mediator assigned to hold this session today. Michael and Sondra, I welcome you both to the mediation center. Let me explain the ground rules. First, I remain neutral—I do not take sides. Everything said in mediation is kept confidential. That means what is said in mediation is not discussed outside this room. Each person takes turns talking without interruption. You are expected to do your best to reach an agreement that considers both your interests. Sondra, do you agree to the rules?

Sondra: Yes.

Mediator: Michael, do you agree to the rules?

Michael: Yeah.

STEP 2: *Gather information*

Mediator: Sondra, tell me what happened.

Sondra: Michael and I were arguing in the hallway. I got mad and threw my books at him. Then he shoved me against the lockers and was yelling at me when Mr. Thomas saw us. Mr. Thomas suspended Michael. I never fight with anyone—I just got so frustrated with Michael, I lost control.

Mediator: You were frustrated and threw your books at Michael. Mr. Thomas saw Michael shove you and suspended him. What did you think when that happened?

Sondra: I felt bad that Michael got in trouble because I started the fight. We aren't talking, and nothing I do seems to help.

Mediator: Sondra, you're sorry Michael was suspended and you're still frustrated. Michael, tell me what happened.

Michael: Sondra is always getting mad at me. She tells everyone on the tennis team I'm rude and selfish. I missed a practice, and she turns it into a war.

Sondra: You're irresponsible. You're either late for practice or you don't even bother to come.

Mediator: Sondra, it's Michael's turn to talk. Please don't interrupt. Michael, you missed a tennis practice, and Sondra got angry. Tell me more about that.

Michael: Well, we're doubles partners. She takes the game much too seriously. She needs to lighten up. She thinks just because she is my tennis partner, I belong to her. She calls me a lot, but I don't want to be with only one girl all the time. I need my space.

Mediator: Michael, are you saying that you are concerned Sondra wants more from you than just being your tennis partner?

Michael: Yes. She doesn't want me to be with other girls.

Mediator: Sondra, do you have anything else you want to add?

Sondra: Michael takes me for granted. I want him to consider how I feel when he stands me up at practice.

Mediator: Sondra, you want Michael to understand your feelings when he doesn't come to practice and doesn't tell you he won't be there.

Sondra: Yes, that's what I want.

Mediator: Michael, do you have anything to add?

Michael: No.

STEP 3: *Focus on common interests*

Mediator: Sondra, why do you think Michael doesn't tell you when he is not going to make practice?

Sondra: Well . . . he probably doesn't want to hear me yell and cry in front of his friends.

Mediator: Sondra, do you think yelling at Michael will help him get to practice?

Sondra: No, I guess not.

Mediator: Michael, what do you want?

Michael: I want her to stop getting so angry.

Mediator: You don't want Sondra to be mad at you. Michael, if Sondra stood you up for practice, how would you feel?

Michael: Oh, I would be worried she got hurt or something. I probably would be mad if I found out she did it on purpose.

Mediator: You'd be concerned that she was all right and upset if she did it on purpose. Michael, what do you really want?

Michael: What do you mean?

Mediator: Do you want to be Sondra's friend?

Michael: I want to be her friend, and I want to be her tennis partner . . . I don't want to be her boyfriend.

Mediator: You want to be Sondra's friend and tennis partner? Is standing her up for practice helping you get what you want?

Michael: No, it's not helping.

Mediator: Sondra, what do you want?

Sondra: I guess I've wanted Michael to be my boyfriend, and the more I try to make that happen the worse things get.

Mediator: Sondra, can you make Michael be your boyfriend?

Sondra: No, not if he doesn't want to be.

Mediator: Sondra, do you want to be Michael's tennis partner?

Sondra: Yes.

Mediator: Do you want to be his friend?

Sondra: I think so.

STEP 4: *Create options*

Mediator: It sounds like you both want to be friends and tennis partners. Now, I want you both to think about what you can do to help solve your problems. We'll make a list of possible solutions by brainstorming. The rules for brainstorming are to say any ideas that come to mind, do not judge or discuss the ideas, and look for as many ideas as possible that might satisfy both of you. Ready? What can you do to solve this problem?

Michael: I could stop skipping practice . . .

Sondra: And let me know if you can't make it.

Michael: We could practice before school if we miss a practice . . .

Sondra: I could stop yelling at Michael.

Mediator: What else can you both do to solve the problem?

Michael: We could play tennis on Saturday mornings and then have lunch together.

Sondra: I could stop calling Michael just to talk.

Michael: I could take the tournament that's coming up more seriously . . . I really didn't think it mattered.

Mediator: Can you think of anything else?

Michael: No.

Sondra: No.

STEP 5: *Evaluate options and choose a solution*

Mediator: Which of these ideas will probably work best?

Michael: Well, practicing before school would work.

Sondra: If I don't yell at Michael and stop calling him all the time, he probably would like practice better.

Mediator: Can you do this?

Sondra: If I get upset about something, I could write Michael a note to explain . . . and then we could talk about the problem instead of arguing. Michael could do the same if he's upset about something.

Mediator: Michael, would this work for you?

Michael: It would be better than yelling.

Mediator: What else are you willing to do?

Michael: Well, we have this tournament coming up . . . I would be willing to practice before and after school and on Saturday mornings to make up for the times I've missed.

Mediator: Sondra, are you willing to do that?

Sondra: That practice schedule would be hard work, but I'll do it. I think we can win if we practice real hard. We also need to let each other know if we need to cancel.

Mediator: How would that work?

Michael: We could either call each other or leave notes in each other's lockers.

Mediator: Sondra, do you agree that would help?

Sondra: Yes.

Mediator: You both agree to practice before school, after school, and on Saturdays. What time?

Sondra: How about at 7:30 and 4:00 during the day and at 10:00 on Saturday?

Michael: OK.

Mediator: You both agree to call or leave a note if you need to cancel practice. You both agree if you have a problem in the future you will write a note to explain the problem and then talk to try to work it out.

STEP 6: Write the agreement and close

Mediator: (Writes up the agreement, then hands it to Sondra and Michael to sign.) Please look this agreement over to be sure it is correct, then sign it. (Sondra and Michael sign, then the mediator signs. Mediator shakes hands with Sondra, then Michael.) Thank you for participating in mediation. Would you two like to shake hands? (Sondra and Michael shake.)

3. After the demonstration, discuss how the peer mediator applied each of the six steps in the process. Explain that the next several activities will describe each step in more detail and give students the opportunity to practice.

7   **Preparing for Peer Mediation**

PURPOSE   Students will learn how to arrange the environment for peer mediation and what materials to assemble before beginning.

TIME   10 minutes

MATERIALS   Student Manual (Reading for Activity 7)
A table and 3 chairs

PROCEDURE

1. Begin by briefly stating the purpose of the activity. Ask students to refer to the reading for Activity 7. Read aloud.

By preparing properly, you demonstrate a sense of control and establish a secure climate in which the disputants are able to communicate. You prepare for the session by arranging the physical environment and assembling materials.

ARRANGING THE PHYSICAL ENVIRONMENT

Arrange the physical environment in the mediation room so that no one is at any kind of disadvantage. Doing so will help the disputants see you as not taking sides and will help them communicate better.

It is important to decide who will sit where before a mediation session begins and to arrange the chairs before the disputants arrive. In arranging the chairs, follow two guidelines.

▲ Position the disputants face to face across from each other.

▲ Position yourself at the head of the table between the disputants and nearest to the exit.

---

2. Ask for two student volunteers to assist in a demonstration by playing the role of disputants. With the volunteers, demonstrate the various seating arrangements illustrated in Figure 8.

3. After each option is illustrated, discuss with the group any potential problems that might arise from it. Point out that arranging the seating before the disputants arrive prevents questions and that having the peer mediator sit at the head of the table between the disputants and nearest the exit helps the disputants see the mediator as being neutral. In addition, having to go past the mediator may cause the disputants to think twice before leaving the room.

4. Continue with the reading.

Figure 8 Effective and Ineffective Seating Arrangements

Example 1 *(ineffective)*

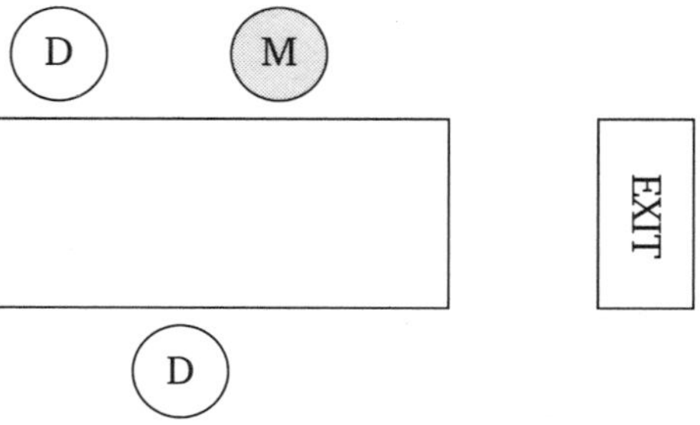

Example 2 *(ineffective)*

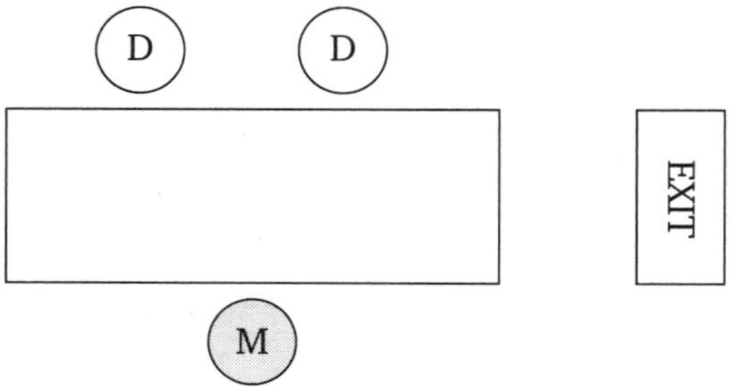

Example 3 *(ineffective)*

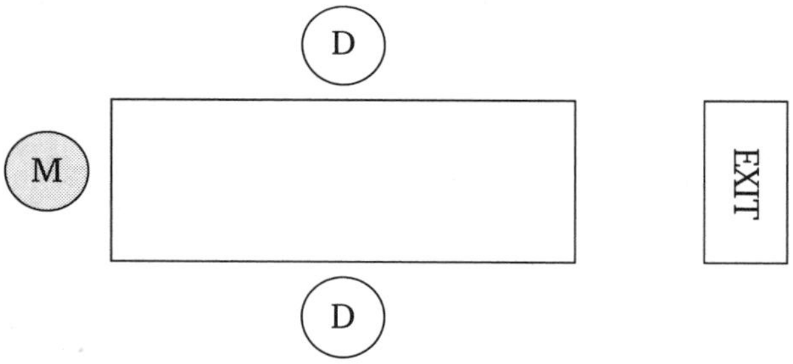

Example 4 *(effective)*

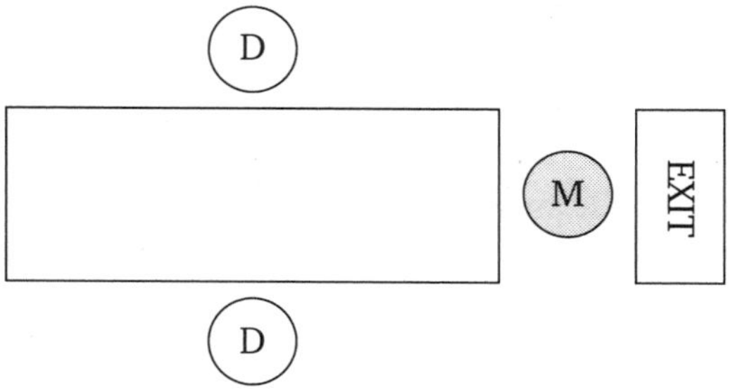

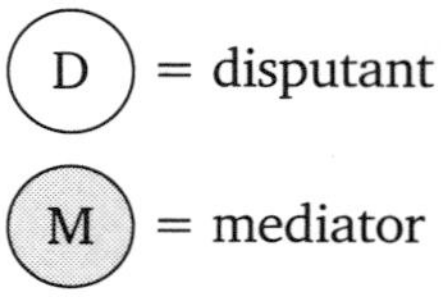

(D) = disputant

(M) = mediator

ASSEMBLING MATERIALS

Before beginning the session, gather the following materials.

- ▲ Peer Mediation Request
- ▲ Brainstorming Worksheet
- ▲ Peer Mediation Agreement
- ▲ Pens or pencils

Copies of these forms appear at the back of your manual.

5. Refer students to the Peer Mediation Forms section in their manuals and have them review the Peer Mediation Request, the Brainstorming Worksheet, and the Peer Mediation Agreement. (Copies of these forms are also provided in Appendix C of this Program Guide.)

PURPOSE   Students will learn how to open the peer mediation session and will have an opportunity to practice this step.

TIME   15 minutes

MATERIALS   Student Manual (Reading for Activity 8)

PROCEDURE

1. Briefly explain that you will be demonstrating how to open the peer mediation session and ask for two student volunteers to play the role of disputants.

2. Ask students to refer to the reading for Activity 8 as the demonstration proceeds.

STEP 1: OPEN THE SESSION

An effective opening sets the stage for the rest of the peer mediation session. You open the session by making introductions, stating the ground rules, and getting a commitment to follow the rules.

1. *Make introductions.*

▲ Introduce yourself.
  ("I am _____. I am your mediator.")

▲ Ask each disputant for his or her name.

▲ Welcome disputants to the mediation center.

2. *State the ground rules.*

▲ Mediators remain neutral.
  ("I am neutral—I do not take sides.")

▲ Mediation is confidential.
  ("Everything said in mediation is confidential. That means nothing said here will go beyond this room.")

▲ Interruptions are not allowed.
  ("Each person takes turns talking without interruption.")

▲ Disputants must cooperate.
  ("You will do your best to reach an agreement that considers both your interests.")

3. *Get a commitment to follow the ground rules.*
  ("Do you agree to follow these rules?")

3. After the demonstration, stress the following points.

   ▲ The ground rules structure a win-win climate.

   ▲ A clear understanding of the ground rules is necessary for the success of the peer mediation process.

   ▲ It is important for the disputants to know that the peer mediator is there to help them create a solution to their problem and not to judge who is right or wrong.

4. Tell the students to divide into groups of three and practice Step 1. Have the students decide who will play mediator first, second, and third. When students are in the role of disputants, they will observe the mediator and give feedback on what the mediator did well or could improve.

5. In the larger group, discuss any questions about opening the session. Summarize by repeating that an effective opening sets the stage for the rest of the peer mediation session.

PURPOSE	Students will learn how to gather information from both sides in order to define the problem in a conflict situation.
TIME	40 minutes
MATERIALS	Student Manual (Reading for Activity 9) Role-Play Handouts for each group of three students (Situations 1, 2, and 3; see Appendix B)

PROCEDURE

1. Briefly state the purpose of the activity.

2. With your co-trainers, present the following mediation demonstration.

Red Riding Hood Versus the Wolf

Mediator: Hello, I am _____. I am your mediator. What is your name?*

Red: I'm Red Riding Hood. They used to call me Little Red Riding Hood, but they don't anymore. You see, the Wolf and I have had this problem a long time, and I grew up.

Mediator: What is your name?

Wolf: I'm the Wolf.

Mediator: Welcome to the mediation center. I'm sorry it took you so long to find us. The ground rules that make mediation work are as follows: I remain neutral—I do not take sides. Everything said in mediation is confidential. Each person takes turns talking without interruption. Finally, you will do your best to reach an agreement that considers both your needs. Red Riding Hood, do you agree to the ground rules?

Red: Yes.

Mediator: Wolf, do you agree to the ground rules?

Wolf: Yes, I do.

Mediator: Red Riding Hood, please tell what happened.

Red: Well, you see, I was taking a loaf of fresh bread and some cakes to my grannie's cottage on the other side of the woods. Grannie wasn't well, so I

---

* Adapted from *Individual Development: Creativity* by Leif Fearn, 1974, San Diego, CA: Education Improvement Associates.

thought I would pick some flowers for her along the way. I was picking the flowers when the Wolf jumped out from behind a tree and started asking me a bunch of questions. He wanted to know what I was doing and where I was going, and he kept grinning this wicked grin and smacking his lips together. He was being so gross and rude. Then he ran away.

Mediator: You were taking some food to your grandmother on the other side of the woods and the Wolf appeared from behind the tree and frightened you.

Red: Yes, that's what happened.

Mediator: Wolf, please tell what happened.

Wolf: The forest is my home. I care about it and try to keep it clean. One day, when I was cleaning up some garbage people had left behind, I heard footsteps. I leaped behind a tree and saw a girl coming down the trail carrying a basket. I was suspicious because she was dressed in this strange red cape with her head covered up as if she didn't want anyone to know who she was. She started picking my flowers and stepping on my new little pine trees. Naturally, I stopped to ask her what she was doing and all that. She gave me this song and dance about going to her grannie's house with a basket of goodies.

Mediator: You were concerned when you saw this girl dressed in red picking your flowers. You stopped her and asked her what she was doing.

Wolf: That's right.

Mediator: Red Riding Hood, is there anything you want to add?

Red: Yes. When I got to my grannie's house the Wolf was disguised in my grannie's nightgown. He tried to eat me with those big ugly teeth. I'd be dead today if it hadn't been for a woodsman who came in and saved me. The Wolf scared my grannie—I found her hiding under the bed.

Mediator: You are saying the Wolf put on your grannie's nightgown so you would think he was your grannie and that he tried to hurt you?

Red: I said he tried to eat me.

Mediator: So you felt he was trying to eat you. Wolf, do you have anything to add?

Wolf: Of course I do. I know this girl's grannie. I thought we should teach Red Riding Hood a lesson for prancing on my pine trees in that get-up and for picking my flowers. I let her go on her way, but I ran ahead to her grannie's cottage. When I saw Grannie, I explained what happened and she agreed her granddaughter needed to learn a lesson. Grannie hid under the bed, and I dressed up in Grannie's nightgown. When Red Riding Hood came in the bedroom, she saw me in the bed and said something nasty about my big ears. I've been told my ears are big before, so I tried to make the best of it by saying big ears help me hear her better. Then she made an insulting crack about my bulging eyes. This one was really hard to blow off because she sounded so nasty. Still, I make a policy to turn the other cheek, so I told her my big eyes help me to see her better. Her next insult about my big teeth really got to me. You see, I'm quite sensitive about them. I know when she made fun of my teeth I should have had better control, but I leaped from the bed and growled that my teeth would help me to eat her.

Mediator: So you and Grannie tried to play a trick on Red Riding Hood to teach her a lesson. Explain more about the eating part.

Wolf: Now, let's face it. Everyone knows no wolf could ever eat a girl, but crazy Red Riding Hood started screaming and running around the house. I tried to catch her to calm her down. All of a sudden the door came crashing open, and a big woodsman stood there with his axe. I knew I was in trouble . . . there was an open window behind me, so out I went. I've been hiding ever since. There are terrible rumors going around the forest about me. Red Riding Hood calls me the Big Bad Wolf. I'd like to say I've gotten over feeling bad, but the truth is I haven't lived happily ever after. I don't understand why Grannie never told my side of the story.

Mediator: You're upset about the rumors and have been afraid to show your face in the forest. You're also confused about why Grannie hasn't set things straight and has let the situation go on for this long.

Wolf: It just isn't fair. I'm miserable and lonely.

Mediator: Red Riding Hood, would you tell us more about Grannie?

Red: Well, Grannie has been sick—and she's been getting a little senile lately. When I asked her how she came to be under the bed she said she couldn't remember a thing that had happened.

3. After the demonstration, discuss by asking the following questions.

   ▲ What did you learn by watching this role-play?

   ▲ How would you define Red Riding Hood's problem?

   ▲ How would you define the Wolf's problem?

   ▲ What did the mediator do to get this information?

4. Ask students to refer to the reading for Activity 9 in their manuals. Read aloud.

STEP 2: GATHER INFORMATION

In this step, you will use the communication skills of *active listening*, *summarizing*, and *clarifying* to help you understand the disputants' situation and feelings and to help the disputants understand how each perceives the problem. These communication skills are discussed in the reading for Activity 5.

1. *Ask each disputant for his or her side of the story.*
   ("Please tell what happened.")

2. *Listen, summarize, clarify.*

3. *Repeat the process by asking for additional information.*
   ("Is there anything you want to add?")

4. *Listen, summarize, clarify.*

---

5. Stress the importance of using the communication skills of active listening, summarizing, and clarifying while gathering information (see Activity 5). Review these skills as necessary.

6. Next divide students into groups of three and explain that each group will perform Role-Plays 1, 2, and 3, rotating the student who plays the peer mediator in each situation. Give the student playing the mediator the sample Peer Mediation Request; the two disputants each receive half of the handout describing the nature of the conflict.

7. A co-trainer assigned to each group of three assists students in role-playing Steps 1 and 2. After each role-play, the co-trainer asks the student who has taken the peer mediator role the following questions to help process the activity.

▲ What did you do well in the role-play?

▲ What could you do differently?

Step 3: Focus on Common Interests

PURPOSE	Students will learn the importance of paying attention to disputants' common interests, not the positions they take.
TIME	Part I: 30 minutes Part II: 60 minutes
MATERIALS	Student Manual (Reading for Activity 10) An orange A knife Role-Play Handouts for each group of three students (Situations 4, 5, and 6; see Appendix B)

PROCEDURE

Part I

1. Hold up the orange and tell the following story.

Half an Orange

Sam and Ben were twins who usually got along fine. One day, however, they got into a terrible fight about who would have the last orange in the bag. Finally, they went to their mother for help in solving their problem. Being a fair mother, she cut the orange in half and gave one half to Sam and the other half to Ben. (Cut the orange in half to illustrate.) The children began to argue again, each demanding the other's half of the orange. The mother could not figure out why. She thought cutting the orange in half was a good compromise.

Stop and ask the students the following questions.

▲ What mistake did the mother make here?

▲ Why did the solution not work?

2. Continue with the story.

When the mother finally realized that she had made a mistake, she asked Ben what was wrong. Ben sobbed that half an orange was not enough to make orange juice. Then Sam cried that there was not enough peel in half an orange to use in the orange rolls he planned to bake.

Stop and ask the following questions.

▲ What are Ben's interests?

▲ What are Sam's interests?

▲ What have you learned from this story?

3. Briefly explain the purpose of the activity, then go on to say that people often take a *position* when they have a problem. In most cases, it is difficult to find any type of solution by focusing only on positions. A temporary agreement may be reached, but such agreements typically do not last because the real interests of the disputants have not been addressed. For lasting solutions, the mediator must get the disputants to focus on their common interests, not their positions.

4. Stress that during the questioning process of Step 3, the peer mediator continues to actively listen, summarize, and clarify the interests of each person (see Activity 5). Ask students to refer to the Identifying Common Interests worksheet in the reading for Activity 10. A copy of this worksheet, with sample responses, is illustrated in Figure 9. Discuss the response to the first example, then have students form groups of six to complete the remaining four examples.

5. When students have completed the exercise, have them reassemble as a large group. Ask each group to share what they feel are the disputants' positions and potential common interests. Point out that many disputes involve multiple interests and that, when disputants are able to acknowledge that each other's interests are part of the problem, they can begin to cooperate.

6. Refer students to the beginning of the reading for Activity 10. Read aloud.

STEP 3: FOCUS ON COMMON INTERESTS

In this step, your goal is to search for interests that join both disputants. **Common interests** serve as the building blocks for an agreement. Unless common interests are identified, disputants probably will not be able to make an agreement they can both keep. Do not move on to Step 4 until you find out what the common interests are.

1. **Determine the interests of each disputant by asking one or more of the following questions.**

   ▲ What do you want?

   ▲ If you were in the other person's shoes, how would you feel? What would you do?

   ▲ Is *(Example: fighting)* getting you what you want?

   ▲ What will happen if you do not reach an agreement?

   ▲ Why has the other disputant not done what you expect?

2. **State the common interests by saying something like the following.**

   ▲ Both of you seem to agree that . . .

   ▲ It sounds like each of you wants . . .

Part II

7. In this portion of the activity, demonstrate Step 3 by role-playing with your co-trainers the first example from the Identifying Common Interests worksheet. Before beginning the demonstration, give the following background: Tyrone found out about the job because he saw Marcus dressed up for the interview and asked him where he was going. Marcus is mad because there is only one job opening and he applied first. Marcus has threatened to fight Tyrone if Tyrone doesn't call and say he is no longer interested in the job.

Figure 9 Sample Identifying Common Interests Worksheet

Directions: Identify the possible positions and common interests the disputants have in the following examples.

Situation	Position	Common Interests
1. Marcus shouts at Tyrone, "You can't apply for the same job I did. There's only one opening, and I was there first!" Tyrone yells, "I deserve that job, too!"	*Marcus wants the job. Tyrone wants the job.*	*Marcus and Tyrone want money, and they also want to be friends.*
2. Lisa yells at her sister, Kara, "You can't ride my bike to school anymore. It's never here when I want it!" Kara yells, "I'm riding your bike—you almost never use it!"	*Lisa won't let Kara ride her bike. Kara will ride the bike.*	*Lisa and Kara both want transportation.*
3. Diana is mad at her boyfriend, Jerome, and says, "If you go out with Emma, I'll never speak to you again." Jerome yells back, "Emma is a friend. I'm not her boyfriend!"	*Diana wants Jerome to go out only with her. Jerome wants to be friends with Emma.*	*Diana and Jerome want to continue their relationship.*
4. James is upset with Malcom: "If you keep asking me for answers in math class, I'll report you to the teacher." Malcom shouts, "Go ahead—I'll report you when you ask me answers in science!"	*James will report Malcom. Malcom will report James.*	*Both James and Malcom want to achieve in math class.*
5. Keisha says to Natalie, "You can't go on the canoe trip because you can't swim like the rest of us." Natalie cries, "I don't need to swim like you. I'm going anyway!"	*Keisha says Natalie can't go on the trip. Natalie is going on the trip.*	*Both Keisha and Natalie want to be a part of the group.*

Marcus and Tyrone's Conflict

Mediator: Marcus, why do you think Tyrone has not withdrawn his application for the job?

Marcus: He really wants a job.

Mediator: Tyrone, if you were in Marcus's shoes, why would you want this job so much?

Tyrone: For the money. We both really need spending money.

Mediator: Marcus, is fighting over this one job helping you get spending money?

Marcus: No.

Mediator: Is fighting helping your friendship?

Tyrone: No, it isn't.

Mediator: What do you really want?

Marcus: I want a job so I'll have spending money.

Tyrone: I want the same.

Mediator: It sounds as though each of you agree that fighting and getting mad isn't good for your friendship or helping you get a job. You both agree that you want a job so you'll have spending money.

8. Next divide students into groups of three and explain that each group will perform Role-Plays 4, 5, and 6, rotating the student who plays the peer mediator in each situation. Give the student playing the mediator the sample Peer Mediation Request; the two disputants each receive half of the handout describing the nature of the conflict.

9. A co-trainer assigned to each group of three assists students in role-playing Steps 1, 2, and 3. After each role-play, the co-trainer asks the student who has taken the peer mediator role the following questions to help process the activity.

   ▲ What did you do well in the role-play?

   ▲ What could you do differently?

   ▲ What questions seemed to help you understand the disputants' common interests?

10. Summarize the main point of this activity by restating that common interests are the building blocks of the resolution. The mediator does not move on to Step 4 until common interests are found.

PURPOSE   Students will learn how to create as many options as possible to solve the identified problem. Brainstorming will be illustrated as a technique of conflict resolution in which disputants, through cooperation and mutual respect, generate solutions that can potentially meet both parties' needs.

TIME   30 minutes

MATERIALS   Student Manual (Reading for Activity 11)
Newsprint
Markers
A copy of the Brainstorming Worksheet for each group of 4 to 6 students
(see Appendix C)

PROCEDURE

1. Briefly describe the purpose of the activity and define *brainstorming* as a technique used to help people come up with as many ideas as possible to solve a problem.

2. Refer students to the reading for Activity 11 in their manuals. Read aloud.

STEP 4: CREATE OPTIONS

Many possible solutions exist for resolving a conflict. However, when we are upset or frustrated, we often do not consider all of our options. In this step, you will help disputants create, through **brainstorming**, a number of options that could potentially solve their problem.

1. Explain to disputants that a brainstorming process will be used to find solutions that satisfy both parties.

2. State the rules for brainstorming.

   ▲ Say any ideas that come to mind.

   ▲ Do not judge or discuss the ideas.

   ▲ Come up with as many ideas as possible.

3. Help the brainstorming process along by using the following questions.

   ▲ What could be done to resolve this dispute?

   ▲ What other possibilities can you think of?

   ▲ In the future, what could you do differently?

4. Write the disputants' ideas on a Brainstorming Worksheet.

---

3. To demonstrate how brainstorming works, ask students to divide into groups of 4 to 6 members each. Give each group a sheet of newsprint and a marker and ask them to draw a brick at the top of their newsprint. Tell them that they have 3 minutes to conduct a "brick brainstorm"—that is, to come up with as many uses for a brick as they can.

4. After the time is up, ask each group to share the number of ideas they came up with and their two or three most unusual uses for the brick. (If desired, you can repeat this exercise with another object, such as a paper clip.)

5. Next pass out a copy of the Brainstorming Worksheet to each group. Assign each group one of the six role-play situations already practiced; have groups come up with 7 to 10 possible options for solving the conflict.

   ▲ Role-Play 1: Two students are in conflict because one of them keeps cutting into the lunchline

   ▲ Role-Play 2: Two locker partners are arguing about missing things

   ▲ Role-Play 3: Two students had a loud disagreement in class

   ▲ Role-Play 4: Two students were ready to fight in the cafeteria

   ▲ Role-Play 5: Two students were fighting in the locker room

   ▲ Role-Play 6: Two students are very mad at each other because of a lost library book

6. Ask each small group to report to the larger group on the options they generated to solve their assigned conflict. Discuss the following questions.

   ▲ Was it hard to follow the rules for brainstorming?

   ▲ Did some of the options seem ridiculous?

   ▲ When did the best ideas come out?

   ▲ Was there much silence? If so, how did you handle it?

7. Summarize by asking students to identify the most important thing they learned in this activity.

12 Step 5: Evaluate Options and Choose a Solution

PURPOSE   Students will learn how to help disputants choose the best option from those generated in Step 4 and how to check that option to be sure it is sound.

TIME   30 minutes

MATERIALS   Student Manual (Reading for Activity 12)
Completed Brainstorming Worksheets from Activity 11

PROCEDURE

1. Briefly describe the purpose of the activity, then refer students to the reading for Activity 12 in their manuals. Read aloud, then briefly discuss.

STEP 5: EVALUATE OPTIONS AND CHOOSE A SOLUTION

Your main task in this step is to **help the disputants evaluate and improve on the ideas** they brainstormed in Step 4. It is also important to check the solution to be sure it is sound. If the solution is not sound, you will need to help the disputants work out a better one.

1. ***Ask disputants to nominate ideas or parts of ideas that seem to have the best possibilities of working.***

2. ***Circle these ideas on the Brainstorming Worksheet.***

3. ***Evaluate options circled and invent ways to improve the ideas by using one or more of the following questions.***

    ▲ What are the consequences of deciding to do this?

    ▲ Is this option a fair solution?

    ▲ Does it address the interests of everyone involved?

    ▲ Can it be done?

    ▲ What do you like best about the idea?

    ▲ How could you make the idea better?

    ▲ What if one person did _____? Could you do _____?

    ▲ What are you willing to do?

---

4. When an agreement is reached, check to be sure it is sound by answering the following questions.

▲ Is the agreement *effective?*
(Does the agreement resolve the major concerns and issues each disputant has? Will the agreement help if the problem reoccurs?)

▲ Is the agreement *mutually satisfying?*
(Do both disputants think the agreement is fair?)

▲ Is the agreement *specific?*
(Can you answer who, what, when, where, and how?)

▲ Is the agreement *realistic?*
(Is the plan reasonable? Can it be accomplished?)

▲ Is the agreement *balanced?*
(Does each person agree to be responsible for something?)

5. Summarize the agreement.
("You are both agreeing to . . .")

2. After reviewing Step 5 procedures, have the students return to the brainstorming groups they formed in Activity 11 and review their previously completed Brainstorming Worksheets. Instruct the groups to choose one or more options that they believe would solve their assigned conflict. (Some groups might want to combine options.) Have students evaluate their solution to be sure it is sound.

3. After about 5 minutes, have each group report their decision to the larger group. Discuss and give feedback.

13

Step 6: Write the Agreement and Close

PURPOSE   Students will learn how to formalize the verbal agreement between disputants as a written statement and how to close the session.

TIME   Part I: 30 minutes
Part II: 60 minutes

MATERIALS   Student Manual (Reading for Activity 13)
Completed Brainstorming Worksheets (from Activities 11 and 12)
Copy of the Peer Mediation Agreement for each brainstorming group
   (see Appendix C)
Role-Play Handouts for each group of three students
   (Situations 7, 8, and 9; see Appendix B)

PROCEDURE

Part I

1. Briefly state the purpose of the activity, then refer students to the reading for Activity 13 in their manuals. Read aloud.

STEP 6: WRITE THE AGREEMENT AND CLOSE

Writing the agreement at the end of the peer mediation session further clarifies the disputants' responsibility for resolving the conflict. In addition, the written agreement serves as a record of what was decided in case future questions arise.

The peer mediator closes the session by shaking hands with the disputants, having the disputants shake hands, and thanking them for participating in mediation. These gestures symbolize mutual respect and promote cooperation.

1. *Write the agreement reached by the disputants on the Peer Mediation Agreement form.*

2. *Ask each disputant to sign the agreement. Then sign the agreement yourself.*

3. *Shake hands with each person and congratulate the person for working to reach an agreement.*

4. *Ask both of the disputants to shake hands.*

5. *Close by saying, "Thank you for participating in mediation."*

---

2. Refer students to the Sample Peer Mediation Agreement included in their reading and discuss. (This form is shown in Figure 10.)

Figure 10 Sample Peer Mediation Agreement

Peer mediator ___Rodney Anderson___ Date ___2/15/92___

Briefly describe the conflict: ___Andrew borrowed Heather's Walkman and took it into school even___
___though Heather asked him not to do it. The principal confiscated the Walkman.___

_____

_____

_____

_____

Type of conflict (check one) ☐ Rumor ☐ Threat ☐ Name-calling ☐ Fighting
☑ Loss of Property ☐ Other (specify) _____

The students whose signatures appear below met with a peer mediator and with the assistance of the mediator reached the following agreement.

Disputant ___Heather___

Agrees to ___Act calmer and not yell at Andrew if a problem happens in the future. She will talk with___
___Andrew first to check things out and will not jump to conclusions.___

_____

Disputant ___Andrew___

Agrees to ___Talk with the principal today to see if he can get Heather's Walkman. If he cannot, he will___
___ask if the principal will accept Andrew's Walkman in place of Heather's. Then he will return Heather's___
___Walkman to her.___

We have made and signed this agreement because we believe it resolves the issue(s) between us

Andrew Smith	_Heather Jones_
Disputant signature	Disputant signature
Rodney Anderson	_15_
Peer mediator signature	Length of mediation (r

3. Ask students to divide into the brainstorming groups they formed earlier in Activities 11 and 12. Give each group a blank copy of the Peer Mediation Agreement and ask them to work together to write up the agreement they chose as a solution to their assigned conflict. Provide assistance as necessary.

Part II

4. In this part of the activity, divide students into groups of three and explain that each group will perform Role-Plays 7, 8, and 9, rotating the student who plays the peer mediator in each situation. Give the student playing the mediator the sample Peer Mediation Request; the two disputants each receive half of the handout describing the nature of the conflict.

5. A co-trainer assigned to each group of three assists students in role-playing Steps 1 through 6. After each role-play, the co-trainer asks the student who has taken the peer mediator role the following questions to help process the activity.

   ▲ What did you do well in the role-play?

   ▲ What could you do differently?

6. Discuss the role-plays and any questions in the larger group.

14   **Supporting Yourself and Others**

PURPOSE   This activity is based on the expectation that peer mediators must support them-selves and others throughout the process. Students will discuss problems that might arise in peer mediation and will sign the Peer Mediator Contract.

TIME   30 minutes

MATERIALS   Student Manual (Reading for Activity 14)
Copy of the Peer Mediator Contract for each student (see Appendix C)

PROCEDURE

1. Refer students to the reading for Activity 14. Read aloud.

> Being a peer mediator is not always easy, but it is always a challenge. It is important to be positive and optimistic even though a mediation is difficult or the outcome is not as you expect. Remember, you are there only to offer your skilled assistance.
>
> ▴ ***The problem belongs to the disputants—they own it and are the only ones who can solve it.***
>
> The times when mediations seem difficult or frustrating can become times of growth and change for everyone. Take the opportunity to talk with other peer mediators or adult staff members and share your thoughts and feelings.
>
> ▴ ***If there is honest communication, thinking will be expanded and boundaries will be broken.***
>
> Encouraging another's efforts, sharing perspectives, and cooperating to solve human problems is a lifelong challenge. Through mutual support and respect, everyone will become stronger and better able to reach common goals.
>
> ▴ ***As Gandhi said, "If we are to reach real peace in this world, we shall have to begin teaching cooperation to the children."***

2. Ask students for examples of how the peer mediator can increase trust and communication and how the mediation process can be used to help people reach common goals. Discuss.

3. Give each student a copy of the Peer Mediation Contract. Read it aloud to the students. Have them ask any questions and then sign it as their formal agreement to the basic expectations of the program.

4. Finally, give students time to ask questions about any problems they may be concerned about. Some typical questions and their answers follow.

Q. *What happens if the disputants keep interrupting and getting mad at each other?*

A. If disputants are interrupting, remind them that they agreed to follow certain ground rules for peer mediation, one of which is not to interrupt. The process will not work if communication and mutual respect are not practiced.

Q. *What should I do if the disputants have no idea how to solve their problem? Can I give them ideas?*

A. You will need to encourage both disputants to work together to come up with ideas. They probably have some ideas but just aren't comfortable saying them. It is all right to give a suggestion to get the ball rolling. However, if after you make a second suggestion the disputants still haven't shared any of their ideas, ask them how serious they are about solving the problem.

Q. *What happens if no agreement is reached?*

A. You could try several things. First, you might ask questions to determine whether the problem is really significant or whether a solution has already been worked out. Second, you might try to find out more about the conflict and better define the disputants' common interests. Third, you could recognize that resistance is common in peer mediations and just keep talking—a solution might be close. If after a reasonable amount of time no agreement is reached, you might ask disputants to continue tomorrow. If none of these solutions work, don't feel you have failed. Giving disputants the chance to engage in the process is the important thing.

Q. *What if during a peer mediation things aren't going well and I'm not sure what to do next?*

A. Not every mediation goes as planned. However, if there is a problem, you should return to the basic steps and ask the process questions you have learned. If that doesn't help, ask an adult supervisor for help or suggestions.

Q. *What happens if a mediation agreement is broken?*

A. There will be times when an agreement will be broken. Disputants should be encouraged to try to mediate a second time. Often if an agreement is broken it means that the original resolution did not meet the needs of each disputant. One way to handle more difficult disputes is to have two mediators present. Co-mediation can be done with two peer mediators or with an adult and a peer mediator. Sometimes two heads are better than one.

CHAPTER 6

Peer Mediator Training: Ongoing Support

The core training activities described in chapter 5 will prepare students to tackle most peer mediation sessions. However, it is very important that trainers provide ongoing support and opportunities for learning. One way to accomplish this is by observing peer mediators on a regular basis. Students can be encouraged to assess their own skills by filling out a Peer Mediator Self-Evaluation form after each mediation (see Appendix C). Informal meetings of trainers and peer mediators to discuss particular problems will also be helpful in providing much-needed feedback and support.

Follow-up training after peer mediators have had some hands-on experience is another way to give ongoing support. This chapter outlines five activities that can form the basis for such additional training. The first four activities focus on caucusing, uncovering hidden interests, dealing with anger, and reducing prejudice. The fifth gives students the opportunity to practice an advanced role-play to bring together the information they have learned in this additional training. Figure 11 suggests an agenda for presenting a day-long follow-up training session. As for the core training activities, the times noted are meant as a general guideline.

Figure 11 Sample 1-Day Agenda: Ongoing Support

Morning

8:30 – 9:00	Boundary Breakers
9:00 – 10:15	Activity 15: Caucusing
10:15 – 10:30	*Break*
10:30 – 11:30	Activity 16: Uncovering Hidden Interests
11:30 – 12:30	*Lunch*

Afternoon

12:30 – 1:15	Activity 17: Dealing With Anger
1:15 – 2:00	Activity 18: Reducing Prejudice
2:00 – 2:30	Activity 19: Advanced Role-Play
2:30 – 3:00	Closure Activities

PURPOSE	Students will learn when and how to caucus in a peer mediation session.
TIME	75 minutes
MATERIALS	Student Manual (Reading for Activity 15) Role-Play Handouts for each group of three students (Situations 10, 11, and 12; see Appendix B)

PROCEDURE

1. Briefly state the purpose of the activity. Refer students to the reading for Activity 15 in their manuals. Read aloud.

Caucusing is a strategy used in special situations to help disputants reach an agreement. Caucusing simply means meeting with each disputant individually. It may take place more than once and at any time during peer mediation, or it may not be used at all. It is the mediator's responsibility to decide whether or not a caucus is necessary.

REASONS FOR CAUCUSING

Caucusing can be used in a number of ways.

- ▲ To uncover information or clarify details that disputants may be willing to give only in private
- ▲ To move beyond an impasse
- ▲ To reduce tension between disputants
- ▲ To explore options
- ▲ To give people time to think alone and reflect
- ▲ To build trust in the peer mediator

GUIDELINES FOR CAUCUSING

1. ***Give both disputants the opportunity to meet individually with you.***
   ("I want to meet with each of you alone.")

2. ***During the individual meetings, use the procedures in Step 2 (gather information), Step 3 (focus on common interests), and Step 4 (create options), depending on the situation.***

---

3. Before returning to the joint session, be sure you have a clear understanding of what information the disputants do not want revealed.
(All statements made during caucusing are confidential unless the disputant agrees that the information can be shared. "Everything said when we are alone is confidential. I will not share anything said with the other disputant unless you give me permission.")

4. When both parties return to the joint session, summarize common interests and return to the step in the process where the disputants were when the caucus was called.

2. Divide students into groups of three and explain that each group will perform Role-Plays 10, 11, and 12, rotating the student who plays the peer mediator each time. Give the student playing the mediator the sample Peer Mediation Request; the two disputants each receive half of the handout describing the nature of the conflict. Explain that the mediator will be expected to use the caucusing strategy during the role-play.

3. A co-trainer associated with each role-play group should take the students playing the disputant roles aside and instruct them in how to play their roles so the mediator will need to call a caucus.

4. After each student plays the peer mediator, the co-trainer should help process the role-play by asking the following questions.

   ▲ What did you do well in the role-play?

   ▲ What could you do differently?

   ▲ What questions do you have about caucusing?

5. Reconvene as a large group and ask the students to discuss the circumstances in which they might use the caucusing strategy. Point out that, although caucusing is rarely necessary in peer mediation, it is a good strategy to use in mediations where disputants are not effectively communicating and where resolution does not otherwise appear possible.

16   **Uncovering Hidden Interests**

PURPOSE   Students will practice identifying the sources of various conflicts and will see how unmet basic needs are the hidden interests that cause most conflicts.

TIME   60 minutes

MATERIALS   Student Manual (Reading for Activity 16)
Index cards
Pens or pencils
Newsprint
Markers
Masking tape

PROCEDURE

1. Briefly state the purpose of the activity, then refer students to the reading for Activity 16 in their manuals. Read aloud.

> You might think determining what is at the bottom of a conflict is an easy matter, but often what the conflict appears to be about is not the only issue involved. People sometimes have **hidden interests** in a conflict situation—and often these hidden interests are unmet basic needs for belonging, power, freedom, or fun.
>
> As mentioned in the reading for Activity 3, conflicts that appear to be about **limited resources** or **different values** are often really about **unmet basic needs**. For example, suppose Robert is upset because his friend LaToya has not repaid some money she borrowed. In this case, you might think the conflict is caused by limited resources (in other words, a lack of money). But when LaToya offers to pay the money back in installments over a few weeks, Robert refuses to accept her solution. In reality, Robert may view LaToya's failure to repay the loan as a lack of respect and feel that his need for **power** is being threatened. The conflict is unlikely to be resolved until Robert's unmet need is recognized. In the mediation session, this recognition could come in the form of an apology from LaToya for not repaying the money as she had first promised.
>
> Or suppose Maria is somebody who places a high value on honesty in friendships. She is angry with her friend Angela because Angela lied to her. In mediation, Maria will not accept Angela's explanations. Is the conflict the result of **different values** about honesty? Maybe yes and maybe no. In this case, Maria may be bothered less by the clash of values than by the fact that she feels she must cut herself off from Angela because Angela lied. In other words, Maria's need for **belonging** may be threatened. If this is the case, any solution to the problem will have to involve helping Maria decide whether she wants to accept Angela as a friend again.
>
> An important part of your job as a peer mediator is to try to figure out what is really causing a conflict. If you do not, the agreements you help disputants reach are unlikely to be lasting ones.

2. Hand out three index cards per student. Ask each student to write a brief description of three conflicts he or she has experienced, one on each card.

3. Next give each group a sheet of newsprint and a marker and ask them to reproduce the diagram shown in Figure 12.

Figure 12 Hidden Interests Diagram

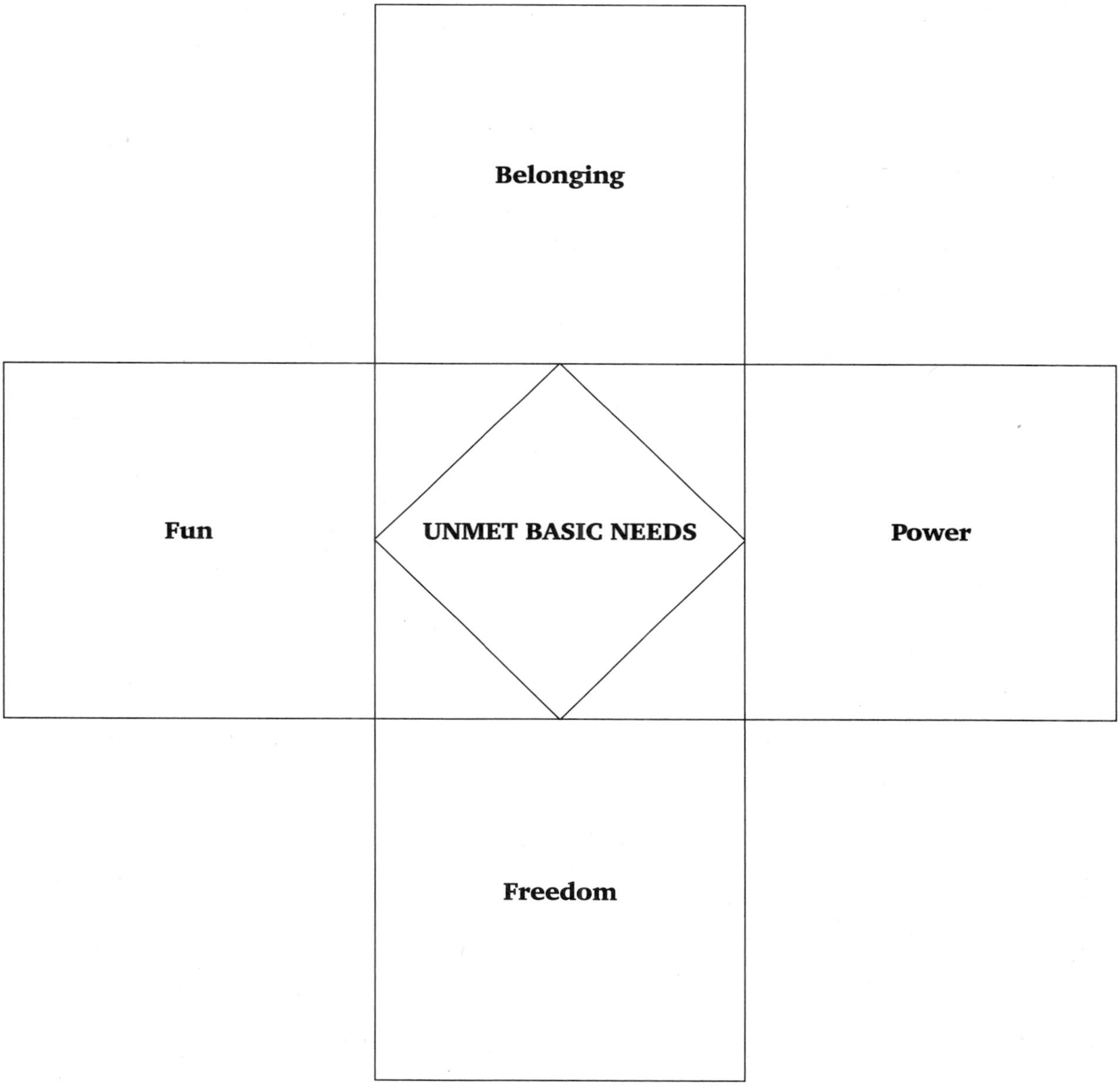

4. Ask each group to pool and shuffle their index cards. Instruct group members to take turns drawing cards from the stack and leading the discussion. As a group, they must decide whether the conflict in any way concerns limited resources or different values, then write on the card *resources* or *values*, as appropriate. They must then determine whether the hidden interest is an unmet need for belonging, power, freedom, or fun and tape the index card to the appropriate area on the diagram. (Cards may overlap areas.)

5. Reconvene as a large group and use the following questions to process the activity.

   ▲ What were some conflicts identified by your group as being related to limited resources? What were the unmet needs associated with them?

   ▲ What were some conflicts identified by your group as being related to different values? What were the unmet needs associated with them?

   ▲ Were there some conflicts related to unmet needs where resources or values were not involved?

   ▲ Were there conflicts that concerned more than one unmet need?

   ▲ What were some conflicts you had difficulty classifying?

   ▲ How did you identify the unmet needs?

   ▲ What have you learned from this exercise?

6. Review the questions from Step 3 of the peer mediation process that help uncover common interests (see the reading for Activity 10). Point out that these questions can also help reveal unmet basic needs.

   ▲ What do you want?

   ▲ If you were in the other person's shoes, how would you feel? What would you do?

   ▲ Is *(Example: fighting)* getting you what you want?

   ▲ What will be the consequences if you do not reach an agreement?

   ▲ Why has the other disputant not done what you expect?

Dealing With Anger

PURPOSE   Students will learn the various ways anger can be expressed and how to identify and deal with two types (aggression and passive-aggression) in the peer mediation session.

TIME   45 minutes

MATERIALS   Student Manual (Reading for Activity 17)
Paper
Pens or pencils
Chalkboard or flip chart
Role-Play Situation (selected from Appendix B)

PROCEDURE

1. Briefly explain the purpose of the activity, then refer students to the reading for Activity 17 in their manuals. Read aloud.

> ***Anger*** is a strong human emotion that is a signal that one or more of our basic needs (belonging, power, freedom, or fun) are not being met. Although most people think of anger as being a negative feeling, it is really neither good nor bad. The way people choose to process their anger can have either positive or negative outcomes, however.
>
> One way to process anger is by ***turning it inward***. The person who behaves this way is often depressed. In addition, because he never expresses his anger, no one ever knows what he thinks or wants. As a result, he rarely gets his needs met.
>
> Another way to process anger is ***aggression***. Being aggressive means verbally or physically attacking another individual. This includes fighting, yelling, name-calling, put-downs, and so forth. Generally, aggression turns people off, or they choose to react in a similarly aggressive way, and the problem just gets worse.
>
> A third way to process anger is ***passive-aggression***. The person behaving this way looks calm on the outside but is really angry inside. She might show anger by rolling her eyes, interrupting, or refusing to cooperate. Others tend to avoid the passive-aggressive person or choose to get angry in return.
>
> Still another way to process anger is ***assertion***. The assertive person knows he is angry and chooses to express that feeling in an appropriate way. He knows what he wants and needs and can ask for it without showing disrespect for other people's wants and needs. Dealing with anger by being assertive makes it much more likely that people will be able to cooperate and reach a mutually satisfying solution.
>
> As a peer mediator, you can help people process their anger through assertion, not aggression or passive-aggression.

2. Ask students to write down the last three times that they were angry, then encourage them to share their examples and the ways they commonly deal with their own anger.

3. Present the following questions for discussion.

   ▲ What do all of these examples of anger have in common?

   ▲ Why do you think people get angry?

   ▲ How do you think unmet needs for belonging, power, freedom, and fun might relate to anger?

4. Ask students to brainstorm a list of ideas for dealing with anger (either aggressive or passive-aggressive) in the peer mediation session. Write the list on the chalkboard or flip chart. After a number of ideas have been generated, go back and discuss each point. The list should include the following suggestions.

   ▲ Remind disputants of the rules (for example, no interrupting).

   ▲ Remind disputants to focus on the problem, not the other person.

   ▲ Use your best listening skills, paraphrase the events and reflect on disputants' feelings, and acknowledge the anger—let disputants know they have been heard.

   ▲ Try to find out the history of the dispute. (Often, strong feelings mean the dispute has been going on a long time.)

   ▲ Tell disputants to relax and take a deep breath.

   ▲ Ask disputants to table the mediation until tomorrow.

   ▲ Caucus with each disputant. Ask disputants what they want. Then ask if anger is helping.

5. With two co-trainers, role-play a dispute selected from the Role-Play Situations given in Appendix B, illustrating first an aggressive response and then a passive-aggressive response. After each role-play, ask students to identify the techniques that were used to deal with the individual's anger.

6. Close by emphasizing that the peer mediation process tries to teach people to handle their anger in an appropriate, assertive way.

18   Reducing Prejudice

PURPOSE   Students will gain a deeper understanding of conflicts that occur over racial and ethnic differences and conflicts that occur simply over lack of respect for individual differences. They will learn how prejudice affects disputes and how reducing prejudice makes resolution possible.

                          NOTE: This activity presents only a very brief look at issues involved in understanding another person's culture. For more about cross-cultural concerns, consult the resources given in the bibliography.

TIME   45 minutes

MATERIALS   Student Manual (Reading for Activity 18)
Two signs, one with the word *alike*, the other with the word *different*

PROCEDURE

1. Briefly explain the purpose of the activity, then refer students to the reading for Activity 18 in their manuals. Read aloud.

> Think of the different types of students who go to your school. Think of their different backgrounds, values, and interests. We are all different—we are different sizes and have different color hair, eyes, and skin. We have different religions and biases. Unfortunately, people often react to these differences with prejudice. When we pre-judge a person because of age, race, sex, disability, or social class, that is prejudice. Prejudice can cause discrimination and oppression, and it keeps people from meeting their basic needs.
>
> Your ethnic background, income, where you live, and how you were brought up make up your **cultural background**. As a peer mediator, it is important for you to understand your own cultural background, biases, and behaviors. To be effective, you must become aware of how you view and interact with individuals who are different from you.
>
> It is your role as a peer mediator to help disputants understand **individual differences**. This understanding is essential to finding common interests. Further, through your sensitivity, you can become a powerful model to help others learn to respect individual differences. This respect promotes cooperation and in turn makes resolution possible.

2. Hang the two signs on opposite walls of the room and ask students to stand. Explain that when you call out an identity, each student should stand by the *alike* sign if the identity fits and by the *different* sign if the identity does not fit. Use the following list of identities, or develop one appropriate for your own school community.

Brown eyes	Skate boarder	Musician
Recycler	Native American	Speaker of two languages
Girl	Asian American	Photographer
Tongue curler	Non-American	Preacher
Tall	Scout	Youngest in family
African American	Dancer	Vegetarian
	Soccer player	

3. Use the following discussion questions to process the activity.

   ▲ What were some of your identities?

   ▲ Which ones were you born into?

   ▲ Which ones did you choose?

   ▲ What ethnic backgrounds are represented in the group?

   ▲ What characteristics do the different ethnic groups share?

   ▲ What makes the ethnic groups different from each other?

   ▲ What are some rewards of belonging to some of the groups you were a part of in this activity?

   ▲ What are some disadvantages of belonging to some of the groups you were a part of in this activity?

   ▲ How did it feel to be different?

   ▲ What is prejudice?

   ▲ Were all the people standing under the *alike* sign really exactly alike?

   ▲ Does a person's appearance have anything to do with what he or she is like inside?

   ▲ What stereotypes are evident here?

   ▲ What are some of the negative effects of these stereotypes?

   ▲ How can you avoid stereotyping?

4. Next select a group of students to leave the room by using as a criterion one of the identities from the list (for example, brown eyes). Include two students not in the identity group. (The selection criteria should not be revealed to the students; identify the students by name only.)

5. After the selected students have left the room, tell the remaining students the criterion you used to make the selection, then have them lock arms and form a tight circle. Tell them that when the other students return they are to let only the two students not in the identity group into the circle. They should not talk to any of the students who are part of the identity group—only to one another and to the two students who do not share the identity.

6. Call the students standing outside back into the room and let them know that each one will have 15 seconds to try to break into the circle. If the person does not succeed, he or she must stand outside the circle. Have each member of the identity group take a separate turn. Only the two nonmembers should be admitted.

7. Discuss the following questions to help process this activity.

- ▲ How did it feel to be a member of the identity group?
- ▲ How did it feel to be different and left out?
- ▲ When a (*Example: brown-eyed person*) tried to get into the circle and failed, how did it feel?
- ▲ Have any of you ever been discriminated against? How did it happen? What did you choose to do?
- ▲ Is it fair to judge people on the basis of group membership or because they are different?
- ▲ How can you avoid being prejudiced?
- ▲ How can differences between various groups lead to misunderstandings and conflict?
- ▲ How do you think prejudice and discrimination affect conflict?
- ▲ How can reducing prejudice make resolution possible?
- ▲ What are some ways the peer mediator can facilitate communication between different groups?

8. Summarize by asking the students what they have learned by participating in this activity.

PURPOSE   Students will have an opportunity to observe and discuss a role-play that uses all of the skills that have been taught. This role-play offers the opportunity to review the peer mediation process and to apply and address principles relating to caucusing, hidden interests, anger, and prejudice.

TIME   30 minutes

MATERIALS   None

PROCEDURE

1. Briefly indicate the purpose of the activity, then select three students to role-play.

2. Ask the group to identify a difficult conflict situation from their experience conducting peer mediations. This situation should involve challenges associated with hidden interests, anger, and/or prejudice. Students will likely have many situations to discuss. However, if they do not, the following example may be used.

Role-Play Example

Background: Ray and Adam are from different racial/ethnic groups and have known each other for 2 years. Ray is from a low socioeconomic neighborhood and gets average to poor grades. Adam is from a middle class background, gets good to average grades, and is on a sports team. Ray feels resentment towards Adam because Adam has expensive clothes and a car. Adam doesn't like Ray's attitudes, especially about dating across the races. Both students are popular and influential with their friends.

Conflict: Adam has been making racial slurs towards Ray for some time. In the halls one day, both students lost their tempers and began to fight. The principal has isolated them until there is a successful peer mediation.

3. Have the students role-play the situation. During the role-play, interrupt or ask for suggestions from other peer mediators as appropriate. If there is no clear resolution to the conflict, disputants could agree that fighting is not helping, that they agree to disagree, and that they will respect each other's differences.

4. After the role-play, discuss the process and ask students to point out how the peer mediator dealt with hidden interests, anger, and/or prejudice.

Program Documentation

SAMPLE PROGRAM PROPOSAL TO DEVELOP A PEER MEDIATION PROGRAM

Overview

In schools, the most typical conflicts between students are rumors, name-calling or put-downs, threats of physical aggression, hitting and fights, and lost or damaged property. Unresolved student conflicts may end up in verbal attacks, hurt feelings, loss of friends, disruptive behaviors, and violence. Clearly, students need to become aware of the advantages of working together rather than against one another to resolve conflicts.

In peer mediation, two or more students in a dispute are given an opportunity through an impartial peer mediator to resolve their differences and find a solution satisfactory to all disputants. Mediation is an effective and nonadversarial tool to resolve conflicts. It is a life skill that can be taught to students and that includes communication, problem solving, critical thinking, and decision making. Mediation empowers students to act responsibly and take control over their own lives. In addition, it enhances self-esteem.

The National Association of Mediation in Education provides strong evidence that (a) mediation is more effective than suspensions or detentions in promoting responsible behavior; (b) mediation reduces violence, vandalism, and absenteeism; (c) mediation reduces the time teachers and administrators deal with discipline problems; and (d) mediation promotes peace and justice in our multicultural world through mutual understanding of individual differences.

Peer mediation programs can transform schools from places where conflicts are handled by traditional means—suspension, detention, expulsion—into places where anger and conflict are accepted as part of life. Students learn how to deal with anger constructively, how to communicate their thoughts and feelings without using violence and abusive language, how to think critically about alternative solutions, and how to find solutions in which all parties can win.

Conflict resolution requires skill. Frequently, those involved in disputes do not have the strategies necessary to work out a positive solution. The general aim of establishing a peer mediation program is to help students learn to deal with their conflicts creatively and constructively. The specific goals of peer mediation are as follows.

▲ To teach students that conflicts can be used as opportunities to grow and learn

▲ To reduce aggressive behaviors between students

▲ To reduce the number of students who are suspended

▲ To improve the overall school climate through improved communication and mutual understanding between individuals

PROGRAM ORGANIZATION AND IMPLEMENTATION

The program will be organized and implemented in four phases.

▲ Phase I: Develop Involvement and Commitment

▲ Phase II: Establish School and Community Support

▲ Phase III: Provide Training for Trainers and Peer Mediators

▲ Phase IV: Implement Program

Phase I: Develop Involvement and Commitment

Advisory committee. Three middle school staff members, the school social worker, the school counselor, and the in-school suspension teacher served as a task force to organize an advisory committee. These individuals have researched other school mediation programs and have taught conflict resolution as part of the school's life skills curriculum.

The advisory committee includes two parents, one administrator, five faculty members, two students, and two community representatives. This group has collaborated to develop a plan for peer mediation and to develop this proposal. Responsibilities of the advisory committee include planning long-range goals, developing proposals, planning student orientation assemblies, selecting peer mediators, organizing training sessions, developing procedures and forms, promoting the program, and assisting program coordinators with record keeping and evaluation.

Program coordinators. Two staff members will be selected to coordinate the peer mediation program. The coordinators will be given one period each day for program tasks. Program coordinators' duties include facilitating meetings of the advisory committee, making assignments, keeping the project on its timeline, and supporting other committee members. Coordinators will also be responsible for general supervision of peer mediators and a final program evaluation.

Phase II: Establish School and Community Support

Staff orientation. All faculty in the school will be provided an overview of the proposed peer mediation program and the mediation process. Interested staff will be invited to participate in training. The timeline for program implementation will be outlined during orientation.

Resources and sponsorship. Program sponsorship will be a joint community-school venture. Business or corporate sponsorship will be pursued to help cover expenses for training and promotion. The school will provide for the indirect staff costs.

Procedures. The advisory committee will determine operating procedures and define the types of conflicts that peer mediators will handle. Procedures developed will relate specifically to hours of operation, the referral process, scheduling of mediation sessions, and the process for conducting the session. Appropriate forms will also be designed.

Student orientation. Groups of fewer than 100 students will be scheduled to attend an informal assembly for one period. During this assembly, a demonstration of a typical peer conflict will be presented by a group of students and followed by a mediation of the conflict. Students will learn that mediation is a peaceful way to resolve conflicts. The mediation process will be explained and described as a voluntary process that teaches mutual respect through clear and direct communication. Students will be told how peer mediators will be selected and trained. In addition, they will be informed about the application process and encouraged to apply if interested.

Peer mediator selection. The advisory committee will review all applications. Selection of a diverse group of 30 peer mediators will be the objective. Student mediators must have the respect of their peers and the ability to be understanding, sensitive, nonjudgmental, and assertive. Parent permission for students to become mediators will be obtained by the principal.

Phase III: Provide Training for Trainers and Peer Mediators

Interested staff and advisory committee members will receive 12 hours of training in conflict resolution and peer mediation procedures. Staff will require 2 days professional leave for training.

Peer mediators will receive 2 days of training prior to the opening of the mediation center. This training will focus on understanding conflict, learning communication skills, and facilitating the six-step mediation process (open the session, gather information, focus on common interests, create options, evaluate options and choose a solution, and write the agreement and close). Training will involve role-plays of peer conflicts that typically would be referred to mediation.

Phase IV: Implement Program

Program promotion. A promotional campaign will be designed by students and volunteers from the advisory committee. This campaign will develop an awareness of peer mediation among students, staff, and parents. The program name will be determined and then advertised through brochures, flyers, posters, pins, T-shirts, and public address announcements. A logo will be developed as part of the promotional effort. The mediation center will have a grand opening, and a mediator recognition event will be scheduled.

Ongoing training and support. Monthly after-school sessions will be scheduled to provide ongoing training for peer mediators. In addition, peer mediators will complete a self-evaluation form each time they conduct a mediation, and an adult supervisor will process the evaluation with the student. Mediators will develop plans to strengthen their skills and have the opportunity to talk with supervisors about their concerns.

Record keeping and evaluation. Records will be kept throughout the year to help evaluate program effectiveness and assess the degree to which program goals are met.

SAMPLE ANNUAL EVALUATION SUMMARY

Common Ground, the peer mediation program at the Urbana, Illinois, Middle School, began in September 1989 and operated through May 1990. During that time, peer mediators resolved 245 conflicts between students.

Records were kept and the information totaled. Information was tallied from school records and from Peer Mediation Request and Peer Mediation Agreement forms. Disputants from 1 in every 10 cases were interviewed a month after the agreement and asked if the process had been satisfactory and if the agreement had held.

Slightly over half of the requests for peer mediation (51 percent) were from students. Other referrals came from teachers (27 percent) and principals (22 percent). Of the disputes resolved, 31 percent were between males and 43 percent were between females. A total of 26 percent were conflicts between males and females. Disputes between white students accounted for 47 percent of the total, while disputes between black students accounted for 26 percent. A total of 27 percent of the conflicts were between students of different races.

The causes of conflict and their resolutions were reported as follows.

Name-calling	26 percent	Resolved at a 98 percent success rate
Rumors	23 percent	Resolved at a 100 percent success rate
Hitting/fighting	16 percent	Resolved at a 100 percent success rate
Other (lost or damaged property, relationship problems, etc.)	35 percent	Resolved at a 93 percent success rate

The number of requests for mediation increased approximately 25 percent from the previous semester. Referrals from administrators almost doubled from the previous year. Both these figures suggest increased support for and perception of the effectiveness of the program.

Role-Play Handouts

This appendix includes 12 role-plays that will help students experience the peer mediation process. Role-playing takes place in groups of three with one participant playing the peer mediator and the other two taking the role of the disputants. You can also use groups of four with two co-mediators.

1. Give the student playing the mediator the sample Peer Mediation Request and instruct him or her to fill in the date and grade level for the two disputants.

2. Cut the role-play sheet in half and give each disputant one set of instructions. Have each disputant fill in the other person's name in the blanks and study the situation for 2 minutes.

3. Start the role-play.

4. Intervene only if the mediator gets off track.

5. End the role-play and discuss the results. The following types of questions will be helpful.

   To mediators: "What did you do well in the role-play?"

   "What was the hardest part of the process?"

   "What could you do differently?"

   To disputants: "What did the mediator do well?"

   "Do you think the agreement would hold?"

   "What might you have done differently if you were the mediator?

6. Process the role-plays with the larger group by asking several role-play groups to report the conditions of their agreement. Ask the group for any other suggestions or comments.

Role-Play 1: Peer Mediation Request

Date _____

Names of students in conflict:

_____ *Disputant A* _____ Grade _____

_____ *Disputant B* _____ Grade _____

_____ Grade _____

_____ Grade _____

Where conflict occurred (check one)

☐ Bus ☐ Classroom ☐ Hallway ☑ Cafeteria ☐ Outdoors

☐ Other (specify) _____

Briefly describe the problem:

_____ *Disputant B cuts in the front of the lunchline every day, and I'm getting mad about it.* _____

_____ *I told the person to stop, but he/she won't.* _____

_____

_____

_____

_____

_____

Mediation requested by (check one)

☑ Student ☐ Teacher ☐ Counselor ☐ Administrator

☐ Other (specify) _____

Signature of person requesting mediation ___ *Disputant A* _____

Role-Play 1: Disputant A

Directions: Write in the other disputant's name in the blank spaces. When the mediation begins, tell your side first.

Situation   Two students are in conflict because one of them keeps cutting into the lunchline. One of them has requested the peer mediation.

Your Position   Every day in the lunchline, _____ cuts in front. The lines are really long, and the rule is no cutting in line. You told a lunchroom supervisor last week, but nothing has changed. You are upset that the person is still cutting in.

Background Information   You think _____ is a bully, but you are not afraid to speak up because a rule was broken.

Role-Play 1: Disputant B

Directions: Write in the other disputant's name in the blank spaces. Tell your side of the story second.

Situation   Two students are in conflict because one of them keeps cutting into the lunchline. One of them has requested the peer mediation.

Your Position   You sometimes have stomach problems, so it takes more time for you to eat. Every day you have a friend who saves a place in line for you. _____ keeps telling everyone that you cut in line, but you know it is necessary for you to have more time to eat.

Background Information   You think _____ has a big mouth and is always minding everyone else's business. Your mother thinks you might have an ulcer and has made a doctor's appointment to check it out.

101

Role-Play 2: Peer Mediation Request

Date _____

Names of students in conflict:

___*Disputant A*_____ Grade _____

___*Disputant B*_____ Grade _____

_____ Grade _____

_____ Grade _____

Where conflict occurred (check one)

☐ Bus ☐ Classroom ☑ Hallway ☐ Cafeteria ☐ Outdoors

☐ Other (specify) _____

Briefly describe the problem:

___*Disputant B keeps taking things from my locker. I'm missing books and homework assignments.*___

___*I even lost some lunch money, and I want it back!*___

_____

_____

_____

_____

Mediation requested by (check one)

☑ Student ☐ Teacher ☐ Counselor ☐ Administrator

☐ Other (specify) _____

Signature of person requesting mediation ___*Disputant A*_____

Role-Play 2: Disputant A

Directions: Write in the other disputant's name in the blank spaces. When the mediation begins, tell your side first.

Situation — Two locker partners are arguing about missing things. One of them has requested the peer mediation.

Your Position — Yesterday you opened your locker and your lunch money and your math book with your completed homework were missing. You received a zero on the homework for the day, and when you asked _____ about it he/she wouldn't say anything.

Background Information — You are a messy person and _____ is very neat. You were friends in the past.

✂ -

Role-Play 2: Disputant B

Directions: Write in the other disputant's name in the blank spaces. Tell your side of the story second.

Situation — Two locker partners are arguing about missing things. One of them has requested the peer mediation.

Your Position — Last week some of your pictures inside the locker were gone, as well as your math book. The locker is always a mess, and you just take the first book you see. You admit to taking the book and the money from _____ because you were not sure whom they belonged to.

Background Information — You are a neat person and have given up on trying to keep the locker clean because _____ is so messy.

Role-Play 3: Peer Mediation Request

Date _____

Names of students in conflict:

_____*Disputant A*_____ Grade _____

_____*Disputant B*_____ Grade _____

_____ Grade _____

_____ Grade _____

Where conflict occurred (check one)

☐ Bus ☑ Classroom ☐ Hallway ☐ Cafeteria ☐ Outdoors

☐ Other (specify) _____

Briefly describe the problem:

___*These two students are always arguing in class and have a lot of hostility towards each other.*___

___*They both agreed to mediation before things get out of hand.*___

_____

_____

_____

_____

_____

Mediation requested by (check one)

☐ Student ☑ Teacher ☐ Counselor ☐ Administrator

☐ Other (specify) _____

Signature of person requesting mediation ___*Teacher*_____

Role-Play 3: Disputant A

Directions: Write in the other disputant's name in the blank space. When the mediation begins, tell your side first.

Situation Two students had a loud disagreement in class. A teacher has requested the peer mediation.

Your Position Another student in your math class is always bugging you. Today _____ looked at you, kicked your desk, and pushed your books on the floor. You are ready to fight.

Background Information Math class is hard for you, and you feel that people put you down in the class.

✂ -

Role-Play 3: Disputant B

Directions: Write in the other disputant's name in the blank spaces. Tell your side of the story second.

Situation Two students had a loud disagreement in class. A teacher has requested the peer mediation.

Your Position You think that _____ is always asking dumb questions that disrupt the class. The whole class has to wait around until the teacher answers him/her.

Background Information You think _____ should be in another math class. You are not very patient with people you think are stupid.

Role-Play 4: Peer Mediation Request

Date _____

Names of students in conflict:

_____*Disputant A*_____ Grade _____

_____*Disputant B*_____ Grade _____

_____ Grade _____

_____ Grade _____

Where conflict occurred (check one)

☐ Bus   ☐ Classroom   ☐ Hallway   ☑ Cafeteria   ☐ Outdoors

☐ Other (specify) _____

Briefly describe the problem:

*Disputant B keeps bugging me and talking about me. He/she even threw food at me*

*in the cafeteria yesterday.*

_____

_____

_____

_____

_____

Mediation requested by (check one)

☑ Student   ☐ Teacher   ☐ Counselor   ☐ Administrator

☐ Other (specify) _____

Signature of person requesting mediation ___*Disputant A*_____

Role-Play 4: Disputant A

Directions: Write in the other disputant's name in the blank spaces. When the mediation begins, tell your side first.

Situation   Two students were ready to fight in the cafeteria. One of the students has requested the peer mediation.

Your Position   _____ sits two tables away from you in the lunchroom. _____ keeps making faces and whispering to friends about you. He/she even throws food at you when no teacher is looking. Today you got so mad you accidentally dumped a slice of pizza in _____ 's lap as you walked by.

Background Information   You were friends with _____ in grade school, but the friendship broke off when _____ began this new school year. You are not sure why the relationship changed.

✂ ---

Role-Play 4: Disputant B

Directions: Write in the other disputant's name in the blank spaces. Tell your side of the story second.

Situation   Two students were ready to fight in the cafeteria. One student has requested the peer mediation.

Your Position   _____ was your friend until this year. You believe he/she acts superior to everyone else and is always putting other people down. You know it was no accident that the slice of pizza dropped in your lap. You want your pants dry cleaned at _____ 's expense.

Background Information   You think _____ is acting this way because he/she is in all advanced classes. You still want to be friends.

Role-Play 5: Peer Mediation Request

Date _____

Names of students in conflict:

    Disputant A _____ Grade _____

    Disputant B _____ Grade _____

    _____ Grade _____

    _____ Grade _____

Where conflict occurred (check one)

☐ Bus   ☐ Classroom   ☐ Hallway   ☐ Cafeteria   ☐ Outdoors

☑ Other (specify) _*Locker room*_____

Briefly describe the problem:

    These two students were pushing and ready to fight in the locker room.

    They are isolated until there is a successful mediation.

    _____

    _____

    _____

    _____

    _____

Mediation requested by (check one)

☐ Student   ☐ Teacher   ☐ Counselor   ☑ Administrator

☐ Other (specify) _____

Signature of person requesting mediation __*Principal*_____

Role-Play 5: Disputant A

Directions: Write in the other disputant's name in the blank spaces. When the mediation begins, tell your side first.

Situation Two students were fighting in the locker room. The principal has requested the peer mediation.

Your Position You and _____were playing around in the locker room yesterday and _____ got mad and started fighting. The PE teacher referred both of you to the principal. You still don't know why _____ got so mad.

Background Information You and _____ have been good friends the last 2 years. Joking around and play fighting is how you often act towards one another.

Role-Play 5: Disputant B

Directions: Write in the other disputant's name in the blank spaces. Tell your side of the story second.

Situation Two students were fighting in the locker room. The principal has requested the peer mediation.

Your Position You have gotten very tired of the way _____ has been treating you. He/she can be such a jerk. _____ is always putting you down and using you as a play punching bag. It was time _____ got some of his/her own medicine.

Background Information You feel everyone is on your case. Your grades were low this semester, you were cut from the basketball team, and your father might be taking a job in another town, so your family might have to move.

Role-Play 6: Peer Mediation Request

Date _____

Names of students in conflict:

___*Disputant A*_____ Grade _____

___*Disputant B*_____ Grade _____

_____ Grade _____

_____ Grade _____

Where conflict occurred (check one)

☐ Bus ☐ Classroom ☐ Hallway ☐ Cafeteria ☐ Outdoors

☑ Other (specify) ___*Library*_____

Briefly describe the problem:

___*I loaned Disputant B a library book I checked out, and he/she lost it.*___

___*Now I'm supposed to pay for it.*_____

_____

_____

_____

_____

_____

_____

Mediation requested by (check one)

☑ Student ☐ Teacher ☐ Counselor ☐ Administrator

☐ Other (specify)_____

Signature of person requesting mediation ___*Disputant A*_____

Role-Play 6: Disputant A

Directions: Write in the other disputant's name in the blank spaces. When the mediation begins, tell your side first.

Situation Two classmates are very mad at each other because of a lost library book. One of them has requested the peer mediation.

Your Position You and _____ are fighting because _____ lost a library book. You are working together on a report and _____ borrowed the book from you and never returned it. You got an overdue notice. If you don't find the book, you're going to have to pay for it.

Background Information You don't have the money to pay for the book. You've done most of the work on the report, and _____ was a good friend.

✂ -

Role-Play 6: Disputant B

Directions: Write in the other disputant's name in the blank spaces. Tell your side of the story second.

Situation Two classmates are very mad at each other because of a lost library book. One of them has requested the peer mediation.

Your Position _____ is saying that you lost the library book. However, you are sure that you returned it before the due date. You feel as though he/she is trying to put the blame of losing the book on you.

Background Information _____ has been a good friend. You have a history of losing and forgetting things, and you don't work very hard at school. However, this time you are sure it isn't your fault the book is missing.

111

Role-Play 7: *Peer Mediation Request*

Date _____

Names of students in conflict:

_____ *Disputant A* _____ Grade _____

_____ *Disputant B* _____ Grade _____

_____ Grade _____

_____ Grade _____

Where conflict occurred (check one)

☐ Bus ☐ Classroom ☐ Hallway ☐ Cafeteria ☐ Outdoors

☑ Other (specify) *All over school* _____

Briefly describe the problem:

_____ *Disputant B is saying he/she is going to kick my butt because I was talking to his/her*

_____ *girlfriend/boyfriend. I don't want to fight, but I will.* _____

_____

_____

_____

_____

_____

Mediation requested by (check one)

☑ Student ☐ Teacher ☐ Counselor ☐ Administrator

☐ Other (specify) _____

Signature of person requesting mediation __ *Disputant A* _____

Role-Play 7: Disputant A

Directions: Write in the other disputant's name in the blank spaces. When the mediation begins, tell your side first.

Situation   Two students are threatening each other because of a rumor about a girlfriend/boyfriend. One of them has requested the peer mediation.

Your Position   You have heard from several other students that _____ was holding hands with your girlfriend/boyfriend at the mall last night. You don't like the idea of someone else messing around with your girlfriend/boyfriend.

Background Information   _____ and you have been friends in the past. You think _____ is a flirt and the cause of your relationship's going bad.

- -

Role-Play 7: Disputant B

Directions: Write in the other disputant's name in the blank spaces. Tell your side of the story second.

Situation   Two students are threatening each other because of a rumor about a girlfriend/boyfriend. One of them has requested the peer mediation.

Your Position   You have heard from several other students that _____ wants to fight you. You don't want to fight, and you don't want to go with _____'s girlfriend/boyfriend.

Background Information   You think _____ doesn't have many friends and is jealous of your popularity.

Role-Play 8: Peer Mediation Request

Date _____

Names of students in conflict:

_____*Disputant A*_____ Grade _____

_____*Disputant B*_____ Grade _____

_____ Grade _____

_____ Grade _____

Where conflict occurred (check one)

[✓] Bus   [ ] Classroom   [ ] Hallway   [ ] Cafeteria   [ ] Outdoors

[ ] Other (specify) _____

Briefly describe the problem:

_____*Disputant B has been telling everybody on the bus something that's none of his/her business.*_____

_____*The person better shut up or else!*_____

_____

_____

_____

_____

_____

Mediation requested by (check one)

[✓] Student   [ ] Teacher   [ ] Counselor   [ ] Administrator

[ ] Other (specify) _____

Signature of person requesting mediation ___*Disputant A*_____

Role-Play 8: Disputant A

Directions: Write in the other disputant's name in the blank space. When the mediation begins, tell your side first.

Situation	One student is upset because another has been spreading the rumor that his/her 16-year-old sister is pregnant. The first student has requested the peer mediation.
Your Position	It is true that your sister is pregnant, but you don't think it is anyone else's business.
Background Information	You think _____ has a big mouth and loves to gossip.

✂ - ✂ - - - - -

Role-Play 8: Disputant B

Directions: Write in the other disputant's name in the blank space. Tell your side of the story second.

Situation	One student is upset because another has been spreading the rumor that his/her 16-year-old sister is pregnant. The first student has requested the peer mediation.
Your Position	You told only one person that the other student's sister was pregnant, and you told because that person asked about it. You heard the rumor from other people.
Background Information	You know the sister and think of her as a friend. You think that _____ doesn't need to be so sensitive about his/her sister's situation—a lot of girls get pregnant.

Role-Play 9: Peer Mediation Request

Date _____

Names of students in conflict:

_____ *Disputant A* _____ Grade _____

_____ *Disputant B* _____ Grade _____

_____ Grade _____

_____ Grade _____

Where conflict occurred (check one)

☐ Bus   ☐ Classroom   ☑ Hallway   ☐ Cafeteria   ☐ Outdoors

☐ Other (specify) _____

Briefly describe the problem:

These two students are ready to fight. They have been loud, rude, and disrespectful to each other as

well as to me when I told them to calm down. I will refer them to the office if mediation is not

successful.

_____

_____

_____

_____

Mediation requested by (check one)

☐ Student   ☑ Teacher   ☐ Counselor   ☐ Administrator

☐ Other (specify) _____

Signature of person requesting mediation ___*Teacher*_____

Role-Play 9: Disputant A

Directions: Write in the other disputant's name in the blank spaces. When the mediation begins, tell your side first.

Situation	Two students are threatening each other and ready to fight. A teacher has requested the peer mediation.
Your Position	You are a new student in school. For the past month, _____ has been saying junk about you and giving you dirty looks. Yesterday, _____ bumped into you in the hall and wanted to fight.
Background Information	You miss a lot of your old friends and want to make some new friends in this new school.

✂ -

Role-Play 9: Disputant B

Directions: Write in the other disputant's name in the blank space. Tell your side of the story second.

Situation	Two students are threatening each other and ready to fight. A teacher has requested the peer mediation.
Your Position	You are angry at _____ because he/she came into the school as a new student and put down all your friends. If that is going to be his/her attitude, there is going to be trouble.
Background Information	You are the informal leader of a large group of students. You have the influence to have the new student accepted or rejected by her/his new peers.

Role-Play 10: Peer Mediation Request

Date _____

Names of students in conflict:

_____ *Disputant A* _____ Grade _____

_____ *Disputant B* _____ Grade _____

_____ Grade _____

_____ Grade _____

Where conflict occurred (check one)

☐ Bus   ☐ Classroom   ☐ Hallway   ☑ Cafeteria   ☐ Outdoors

☐ Other (specify) _____

Briefly describe the problem:

*These two students are angry at each other and calling each other names.*

*A rumor is going around the school they have a drinking problem.*

_____

_____

_____

_____

_____

Mediation requested by (check one)

☐ Student   ☐ Teacher   ☐ Counselor   ☐ Administrator

☑ Other (specify) _*Lunchroom supervisor*_ _____

Signature of person requesting mediation __*Supervisor*_____

Role-Play 10: Disputant A

Directions: Write in the other disputant's name in the blank spaces. When the mediation begins, tell your side first.

Situation One student has been calling another student an alcoholic. The lunchroom supervisor has requested the peer mediation.

Your Position You were sitting in the school cafeteria and _____ came up to you and started yelling that you told everybody he/she was an alcoholic.

Background Information You know that _____ gets drunk most every weekend and mentioned to a mutual friend that you think he/she needs some professional help. You want to be friends with _____ .

✂ -

Role-Play 10: Disputant B

Directions: Write in the other disputant's name in the blank space. Tell your side of the story second.

Situation One student has been calling another student an alcoholic. The lunchroom supervisor has requested the peer mediation.

Your Position You like to party but do not feel that you have a problem with drinking too much alcohol. Two people today called you a drunk and you are getting mad. You believe _____ drinks even more than you.

Background Information One of your family members is a recovering alcoholic and you are sensitive about being called a drunk.

Role-Play 11: Peer Mediation Request

Date _____

Names of students in conflict:

_____ *Disputant A* _____ Grade _____

_____ *Disputant B* _____ Grade _____

_____ Grade _____

_____ Grade _____

Where conflict occurred (check one)

☐ Bus   ☐ Classroom   ☑ Hallway   ☐ Cafeteria   ☐ Outdoors

☐ Other (specify) _____

Briefly describe the problem:

*These two students are mad at each other and want to fight.*

*I hope they can work out their misunderstanding.*

_____

_____

_____

_____

_____

_____

Mediation requested by (check one)

☐ Student   ☑ Teacher   ☐ Counselor   ☐ Administrator

☐ Other (specify) _____

Signature of person requesting mediation ___*Teacher*_____

Role-Play 11: Disputant A

Directions: Write in the other disputant's name in the blank space. When the mediation begins, tell your side first.

Situation	Two students were found in the hall after PE class arguing and ready to fight. A teacher who saw and heard the dispute has requested the peer mediation.
Your Position	In the locker room after PE class _____ came up to you, called you a jerk, and spit on your shirt. You want an apology and you want the shirt to be cleaned.
Background Information	You don't really know this person, but you feel strongly that you want your shirt cleaned. You sometimes have been teased during PE, and this has gone too far.

✂ ---

Role-Play 11: Disputant B

Directions: Write in the other disputant's name in the blank spaces. Tell your side of the story second.

Situation	Two students were found in the hall after PE class arguing and ready to fight. A teacher who saw and heard the dispute has requested the peer mediation.
Your Position	In PE class today _____ shoved you during the game. He/she also shoved one of your friends. After class you told _____ to watch out next time. You didn't spit on him—you spit on the floor. You're not going to apologize or clean his shirt.
Background Information	You think that _____ thinks he is better than anyone else and is looking for a fight with you and your friends.

Role-Play 12: Peer Mediation Request

Date _____

Names of students in conflict:

_____ *Disputant A* _____ Grade _____

_____ *Disputant B* _____ Grade _____

_____ Grade _____

_____ Grade _____

Where conflict occurred (check one)

☐ Bus   ☐ Classroom   ☑ Hallway   ☐ Cafeteria   ☐ Outdoors

☐ Other (specify) _____

Briefly describe the problem:

_____ *Disputant B pushed me and hit me in the hall yesterday.* _____

_____ *I don't want to fight.* _____

_____

_____

_____

_____

_____

Mediation requested by (check one)

☑ Student   ☐ Teacher   ☐ Counselor   ☐ Administrator

☐ Other (specify) _____

Signature of person requesting mediation ___ *Disputant A* _____

Role-Play 12: Disputant A

Directions: Write in the other disputant's name in the blank spaces. When the mediation begins, tell your side first.

Situation   One student hit and threatened another student. The student who was hit has requested the peer mediation.

Your Position   In the hall yesterday _____ came up to you and pushed you against the locker and hit you. Your new notebook was damaged. You didn't do anything.

Background Information   You are on probation, and if you fight back you will be "sent up." The current girlfriend/boyfriend of _____ was going with you, and you still want a relationship with that person.

✂ -

Role-Play 12: Disputant B

Directions: Write in the other disputant's name in the blank spaces. Tell your side of the story second.

Situation   One student hit and threatened another student. The student who was hit has requested the peer mediation.

Your Position   For the past week _____ has been looking at, talking to, and putting a move on your girlfriend/boyfriend. There will be trouble if _____ doesn't stay away.

Background Information   You think that _____ likes to threaten and fight with people. You are happy with your new girlfriend/boyfriend and won't take a chance on losing the relationship.

Program Forms

Peer Mediation Request

Date _____

Names of students in conflict:

_____ Grade _____

_____ Grade _____

_____ Grade _____

_____ Grade _____

Where conflict occurred (check one)

☐ Bus ☐ Classroom ☐ Hallway ☐ Cafeteria ☐ Outdoors

☐ Other (specify) _____

Briefly describe the problem:

_____

_____

_____

_____

_____

_____

_____

Mediation requested by (check one)

☐ Student ☐ Teacher ☐ Counselor ☐ Administrator

☐ Other (specify) _____

Signature of person requesting mediation _____

Peer Mediator Release

Student _____ Grade _____

Teachers: There are times when a peer mediator might be asked to conduct a mediation during class time. The student will be released from class only with your permission. Please indicate on this form if you approve an occasional release for this student.

Period	Subject	Room No.	Approval (Y/N)	Teacher Signature
1				
2				
3				
4				
5				
6				
7				
8				

Peer Mediator: I am willing to stay after school to mediate conflicts. ☐ yes ☐ no

I understand that if I am called out of a class to mediate a conflict, I am responsible for making up any missed work.

Student signature _____ Date _____

127

Peer Mediation Process Summary

Step 1: Open the Session

1. Make introductions.
2. State the ground rules.
   - ▲ Mediators remain neutral.
   - ▲ Mediation is confidential.
   - ▲ Interruptions are not allowed.
   - ▲ Disputants must cooperate.
3. Get a commitment to follow the ground rules.

Step 2: Gather Information

1. Ask each disputant (one at a time) for his or her side of the story.
2. Listen, summarize, clarify.
3. Repeat the process by asking for additional information.
4. Listen, summarize, clarify.

Step 3: Focus on Common Interests

1. Determine the interests of each disputant.
2. State the common interests.

Step 4: Create Options

1. Explain to disputants that a brainstorming process will be used to find solutions that satisfy both parties.
2. State the rules for brainstorming.
   - ▲ Say any ideas that come to mind.
   - ▲ Do not judge or discuss the ideas.
   - ▲ Come up with as many ideas as possible.
3. Help the brainstorming process along.
4. Write the disputants' ideas on a Brainstorming Worksheet.

Step 5: Evaluate Options and Choose a Solution

1. Ask disputants to nominate ideas or parts of ideas that seem to have the best possibilities of working.
2. Circle these ideas on the Brainstorming Worksheet.
3. Evaluate options circled and invent ways to improve the ideas.
4. When an agreement is reached, check to be sure it is sound.

Step 6: Write the Agreement and Close

1. Write the agreement reached by the disputants on the Peer Mediation Agreement form.
2. Ask each disputant to sign the agreement. Then sign the agreement yourself.
3. Shake hands with each person and congratulate the person for working to reach an agreement.
4. Ask both of the disputants to shake hands.
5. Close by saying, "Thank you for participating in mediation."

Peer Mediation Agreement

Peer mediator _____ Date _____

Briefly describe the conflict: _____

_____

_____

_____

_____

_____

Type of conflict (check one) ☐ Rumor ☐ Threat ☐ Name-calling ☐ Fighting

☐ Loss of property ☐ Other (specify) _____

The students whose signatures appear below met with a peer mediator and with the assistance of the mediator reached the following agreement.

Disputant _____

Agrees to _____

_____

_____

Disputant _____

Agrees to _____

_____

_____

We have made and signed this agreement because we believe it resolves the issue(s) between us.

_____   _____
Disputant signature   Disputant signature

_____   _____
Peer mediator signature   Length of mediation (minutes)

Peer Mediator Application

Name _____ Grade _____

Address _____ Phone _____

Please answer the following questions.

1. Why do you want to become a peer mediator?

2. What personal qualities do you have that will help you be a good mediator?

3. What type of conflicts do you think are most frequent around the school?

4. List any other school or community activities you are involved in.

If selected, I agree to attend all required training sessions, some of which may be after school. I will make up all classwork missed due to training during school hours.

Student signature _____ Date _____

Teacher Reference

I recommend _____ for peer mediation.

Comments:

Teacher signature _____ Date _____

Parent Notification and Permission Letter

Dear Parent or Guardian:

Your daughter or son has applied and been selected by a teacher committee to be trained as a peer mediator. Peer mediators are students who, with adult supervision, mediate disputes between fellow students. The students selected are known to be fair, reliable, and good communicators.

Conflicts between students are a part of daily life in schools. Conflicts that are most common include name-calling, rumors, threats, and friendships gone amiss. Mediation is a conflict resolution approach where disputants have the chance to sit face to face and talk, uninterrupted, so each side of the dispute is heard. After the problem is defined, solutions are created and then evaluated. When an agreement is reached, it is written and signed.

The trained peer mediator is the outside third person who leads this process. The mediator does not take sides and keeps all information confidential. Mediation is a skill that involves good communication, problem solving, and critical thinking.

Peer mediators will participate in _____ hours of training.

The dates for training are _____ .

The training will be located at _____ .

If you support your child's desire to become a peer mediator, please sign the attached form and have your son or daughter return it by _____ .

If you have any questions please call _____ at _____ .

Sincerely,

✄ -

(detach and return to _____ by_____)

I give my permission for _____
to participate in training and become a peer mediator.

Parent or guardian signature _____ Date _____

Address _____ Phone _____

131

Peer Mediation Record-Keeping Form

Month _____ Page _____ of _____

Mediation No.	Date	Grade	Sex	Race	Location	Requested By	Type	Time	Signed (Y/N)	Kept (Y/N)
1										
2										
3										
4										
5										
6										
7										
8										
9										
10										
11										
12										
13										
14										
15										

KEY

Location
B = Bus
R = Classroom
H = Hallway
C = Cafeteria
D = Outdoors
O = Other

Requested By
S = Student
T = Teacher
C = Counselor
A = Administrator
O = Other

Type
R = Rumor
T = Threat
N = Name-calling
F = Fighting or hitting
P = Property loss or damage
O= Other

Time (to the nearest 5 minutes)

Signed (was an agreement signed?)

Kept (was the agreement still in force at a 1-month follow-up interview with selected disputants?)

Brainstorming Worksheet

List all the possible options.

- ▲ What could be done to resolve this dispute?
- ▲ What other possibilities can you think of?
- ▲ In the future, what could you do differently?

1. _____

2. _____

3. _____

4. _____

5. _____

6. _____

7. _____

8. _____

9. _____

10. _____

Peer Mediator Contract

As a peer mediator, I understand my role is to help students resolve conflicts peacefully. As a peer mediator, I will do my best to respect the participants of mediation, remain neutral, and keep the mediation confidential.

As a peer mediator, I agree to the following terms.

- To complete all training sessions

- To maintain confidentiality in all mediations

- To responsibly conduct general duties of a peer mediator, including conducting mediations, completing all necessary forms, and promoting the program

- To maintain satisfactory school conduct (this includes requesting mediation before taking other action if I become involved in a conflict)

- To maintain satisfactory grades in all classes and make up any class work missed during training or mediation sessions

- To serve as a peer mediator until the end of the year

Possible actions if these responsibilities are not met are as follows.

- First time: Warning

- Second time: Loss of peer mediator status for 1 month

- Third time: Suspension as a peer mediator

I accept these responsibilities for the school year.

Student signature _____ Date _____

Peer Mediator Self-Evaluation

Peer mediator _____ Date _____

Directions: Place a checkmark (✓) by each step where you did quality work. Place an asterisk (*) by each step where you think the quality could improve.

☐ Step 1: Open the session

☐ Step 2: Gather information

☐ Step 3: Focus on common interests

☐ Step 4: Create options

☐ Step 5: Evaluate options and choose a solution

☐ Step 6: Write the agreement and close

1. What did you do well?

2. If you could do this mediation again, what might you do differently?

3. Were certain steps more difficult for you than others? If so, what could you do to strengthen these steps?

4. Do you have any other concerns or questions?

Staff supervisor _____ Date _____

Comments:

Boundary Breakers and Closure Activities

Boundary breakers are activities designed to offer a low-risk way for groups to get acquainted and work together as a team.* Based on cooperation and communication, they can be used either to relax or to energize a group. Most involve movement and a high level of participation.

Closure activities are designed to review, summarize, and reinforce what has been learned. They provide an important check on how participants are feeling and thinking about the events of the day and help trainers plan future training activities that will be successful. Finally, closure activities affirm the positive qualities and efforts of each participant and act to structure the support individuals need to learn and grow.

These activities are short, usually 10 to 15 minutes long, and require few materials. The few handouts mentioned appear at the end of this appendix.

BOUNDARY BREAKERS

The Line Up

1. Have all the students stand, then ask them to line up in a circle around the room in alphabetical order by first names (for example, Alan, Barb, David, Frank . . . Zoey). The person to the left should have a name beginning with an earlier letter in the alphabet; the person to the right should have a name beginning with a later letter. Encourage the students to move around the room, talk, and cooperate to make the circle follow the pattern.

2. After the circle is complete, have the students go around and introduce themselves.

---

* The Line Up, Send a Letter, The Knotted Rope, The Telephone Booth, and Connections Closure have been adapted by permission from activities appearing in *Boundary Breakers: A Team Building Guide for Student Activity Advisers* by J. Schrader, 1990, Reston, VA: National Association of Secondary School Principals. This resource also contains many other good activities.

3. Have one more line-up. This time, ask students to arrange themselves according to their birthdays. Each student should have someone with an earlier birthday to the left and a later birthday to the right. After the circle is complete, encourage students to go around and tell their birthdays and the number of people in their families.

4. Ask students to return to their seats.

Find Someone Who . . .

1. Give each student a Find Someone Who . . . handout. Have students circulate around the room to collect a different signature for each statement. After 5 to 10 minutes, ask them to return to their seats.

2. Read the list aloud and have students raise their hands if a statement applies to them. You might want to ask follow-up questions—for example, if a number of students have finished reading books last week, you might inquire which books they read.

Interview Guide

1. Give each student a copy of the Interview Guide. Next have each one find someone in the class he or she does not know very well and take about 5 minutes to conduct an interview based on the questions given. When one interview is complete, the interviewer and interviewee switch roles.

2. After the interviews are over, have students introduce their partners to the group and share some information they learned.

Sentence Completions

1. Give each student a copy of the Sentence Completions handout.

2. Next have students get into groups of three or four by drawing their desks or chairs into small circles. Have students share responses by going around the circle, one sentence at a time.

3. After 5 to 10 minutes, reassemble the group and discuss for a few minutes what responses students shared.

What Do We Have in Common?

1. Have students number off so they will be divided randomly in groups of five, then ask these groups to place their desks or chairs together in small circles. Ask each person in the group to introduce himself or herself and share a positive experience that has happened recently.

2. Next have each group make a list of 5 to 10 things that everyone in the group has in common. Encourage groups to be creative and avoid the obvious (for instance, "We are all teenagers"). Some ideas to discuss are food, likes/dislikes, pet peeves, favorite activities or sports, music, and families.

3. After 5 to 10 minutes, reassemble in the larger group and have each small group share their list.

Send a Letter

NOTE: This activity is best for groups under 25. If your group is larger, you can divide it accordingly.

1. Arrange the desks or chairs in a circle with yourself in the middle. Be sure that everyone has a chair and that there are no extra chairs in the circle.

2. Explain the rules of the activity by saying that the person who is in the middle must first say his or her name, then say, "I'm sending a letter to _____ ." The student will then fill in the blank with a specific description like "someone with glasses" or "someone with brown hair."

3. Any group member who fits the description must stand up and sit in another student's chair. The person who is left standing gets to be the next sender.

4. Continue the activity for about 5 minutes.

The Knotted Rope

1. Tie a length of rope with a knot for each group member. (Knots should be approximately 2 feet apart.)

2. Ask each student to hold onto the rope with one hand. After everyone is holding on, ask the group to untie the knots in the rope without anyone's removing his or her hand.

3. After the rope has been untangled, give participants a chance to discuss how it felt to accomplish this task.

The Telephone Booth

1. For each group of 10 students, mark a 3-foot square on the floor with masking tape to indicate the walls of a telephone booth. The object of the game is to get all 10 group members into the telephone booth. Allow groups 2 minutes to figure out the problem.

2. After the time is up, ask students the following questions.

   ▲ Who was the leader?

   ▲ Who gave the most ideas?

   ▲ Whose ideas were accepted?

CLOSURE ACTIVITIES

Closure Lists

1. Have students get into groups of 6 to 8. Give each group a sheet of newsprint and a marker and instruct them to make two lists. One list should include new things that they learned during the day; the other should list what they believe will be the hardest about being a peer mediator and what they feel they want to learn more about.

2. After 10 minutes, encourage each group to share their lists.

Connections Closure

NOTE: This activity works best with groups of fewer than 30. Divide larger groups as necessary.

1. Have everyone get into a large circle. Hold a large ball of string or twine and start the activity by making one positive statement about the day. The statement could be about something you learned or relearned, or about a person you met or got to know better. After making the statement, hold the end of the string and toss the ball to someone else.

2. The person who catches the ball makes a similar statement, holds the string, and tosses the ball to another person.

3. When everyone has received the string and made a statement, a web will be produced. Have everyone continue to hold the string while you point out that we are all part of the whole and all interconnected.

The Quality Line

1. Have students sit in a circle. Go around the circle and ask each person to give one reason why he or she is a good peer mediator. This could be a quality or skill (for example, "I am a good listener").

2. Have them go around a second time and share something that they have learned from being a peer mediator. Point out that peer mediation is a growth process for both disputants and mediator.

Hear Your Strengths

1. Have students get into a circle of six to eight individuals.

2. Choose one person in the group to focus on. Go around the circle and have everyone give that person a positive message about a strength the person possesses. Ask students to make eye contact with and speak directly to the person.

3. Instruct the identified person not to interrupt or say anything until everyone has spoken. The person can then say thank you.

4. Continue until everyone has had a chance to be recognized.

You're in the Bag

1. Have students form groups of eight, then give each group member a small paper bag, eight slips of paper, and a pencil or pen.

2. Instruct each student to write his or her name on the paper bag and then to write a positive note or message to each other member of the group and place the message in the person's bag.

3. After all the messages have been delivered, let participants read the notes.

4. Finally, have each person read one or two positive notes to the rest of the group.

Affirmation Exercise

1. Explain that an affirmation is a positive message that we give to ourselves or to others. We need as many positive messages as we can get, and we can get them through positive self-talk or by receiving affirmations from others.

2. Write some examples of affirmations on chalkboard or flip chart.

   - ▲ You are a good listener and others listen to you.
   - ▲ You respect people and help them work together.
   - ▲ You are trustworthy and honest towards others.
   - ▲ You are objective and supportive of others.
   - ▲ You accept and respect people for their efforts.
   - ▲ You enhance other people's lives.
   - ▲ Life is for the taking.
   - ▲ Your efforts and energies make a difference.

3. Have half of the students sit in chairs in a circle and the other half stand directly behind the seated individuals. Ask each standing person to think of an affirmation. Have the sitting people relax and close their eyes. (If you have some relaxing music, play it at this point in the activity.)

4. Ask the standing participants to touch the shoulders of their sitting partners, lean down, and softly say their affirmation. This is done simultaneously to all sitting participants.

5. The standing people then move on in a clockwise fashion to the next sitting person and softly send them the same affirmation, proceeding around the circle until they return to their starting places.

6. The sitting persons and standing persons switch places, and the exercise continues as before.

7. After the exercise is complete, ask how it felt to receive one affirmation after the next, as well as how it felt to give affirmations. Finally, ask how students think this exercise can help them become better peer mediators.

Find Someone Who . . .

Directions: Find a person in the group who fits one or more of the following statements. Have the person sign his or her name by any statements that are true.

1. Was born in another state _____

2. Likes classical music _____

3. Cries at movies or watching TV _____

4. Refuses to walk under a ladder _____

5. Has used an outhouse _____

6. Finished reading a book last week _____

7. Plays a musical instrument _____

8. Speaks a foreign language _____

9. Plays on a sports team _____

10. Is new to this school _____

11. Is the youngest in the family _____

12. Likes to cook _____

13. Has more than three pets _____

14. Likes to play tennis _____

15. Has a family of more than five _____

16. Likes to dance _____

17. Was born on a holiday _____

18. Likes to roller skate _____

Interview Guide

Directions: Find a person you don't know yet and obtain the following information.

1. What is your name?

2. Who are the members of your family?

3. What is your favorite hobby? How did you get interested in it?

4. What is your idea of a perfect Saturday afternoon?

5. What do you like most about school?

6. What would you change about school if you were principal?

7. What would you do with $1,000?

8. What is the best news you could get right now?

9. What is one of the best things that has ever happened to you?

10. Describe your life 10 years from now. Where will you be living? What will be your job? Will you have a family?

Sentence Completions

Directions: These are some sentences about you. Please finish them with the first thought that comes to your mind.

1. I like to _____

   _____

2. My teachers think I _____

   _____

3. One word that describes me is _____

   _____

4. I worry when _____

   _____

5. I hate to hear people say _____

   _____

6. I am best at _____

   _____

7. I want to learn _____

   _____

8. I sometimes wish _____

   _____

9. I am afraid of _____

   _____

10. I get angry when _____

   _____

Bibliography

Allport, G. (1979). *The nature of prejudice.* Reading, MA: Addison-Wesley.

Banks, J. A. (1975). *Teaching strategies for ethnic studies.* Boston: Allyn and Bacon.

Cole, A. (1978). *Children are children are children: An activity approach to exploring Brazil, France, Iran, Japan, Nigeria, and the USSR.* Boston: Little, Brown.

Covey, S. R. (1989). *The seven habits of highly effective people: Restoring the character ethic.* New York: Simon & Schuster.

Fisher, R., & Brown, S. (1988). *Getting together: Building relationships as we negotiate.* New York: Penguin.

Fisher, R., & Ury, W. (1981). *Getting to yes: Negotiating agreements without giving in.* Boston: Houghton Mifflin.

Glasser, W. (1965). *Reality therapy.* New York: Harper & Row.

Glasser, W. (1984). *Control theory.* New York: Harper & Row.

Glasser, W. (1990). *The quality school.* New York: Harper & Row.

Johnson, D. W., & Johnson, R. T. (1975). *Learning together and alone: Cooperation, competition and individualization.* Englewood Cliffs, NJ: Prentice-Hall.

Kreidler, W. J. (1984). *Creative conflict resolution: More than 200 activities for keeping peace in the classroom.* Glenview, IL: Scott, Foresman.

Pasternak, M. G. (1979). *Helping kids learn multi-cultural concepts: A handbook of strategies.* Champaign, IL: Research Press.

Prutzman, P. (1978). *The friendly classroom for a small planet: A handbook of creative approaches to living and problem solving for children.* Wayne, NJ: Avery.

Rainbow activities: 50 multicultural/human relations experiences. (1977). South El Monte, CA: Creative Teaching Press.

Shuter, R. (1979). *Understanding misunderstandings: Exploring interpersonal communication.* New York: Harper & Row.

Simon, S. B., Howe, L. W., & Kirschenbaum, H. (1972). *Values clarification: A handbook of practical strategies for teachers and students.* New York: Hart.

Stanford, B. (Ed.). (1976). *Peacemaking.* New York: Bantam.

Glossary

ACTIVE LISTENING: Using nonverbal behaviors such as tone of voice, eye contact, and gestures to indicate understanding

AGGRESSION: Forceful action or attack

APOLOGIZE: To admit error or discourtesy by an expression of regret

ARBITRATE: To hear and decide a solution for two parties in controversy

ASSERTION: Expressing one's needs and wants in a way that shows respect for others' needs and wants

AVOID: To keep away from, stay clear of, shun

BASIC NEEDS: Needs that underlie all human behavior (belonging, power, freedom, fun)

BEHAVE: To act, function, or conduct oneself in a specific way

BELONGING: A feeling of being part of a group or in natural association with others (one of the four basic needs)

BIASED: Having a settled and often prejudiced outlook

BRAINSTORMING: A technique for helping disputants create as many options as they can for solving their problem

CAUCUS: Meeting with each disputant individually

CHOICE: Option or selection; power of deciding

CLARIFY: To make clearer or easier to understand

COMBINE: To bring into a state of unity, join, merge, or blend; to join forces for a common purpose or enter into an alliance

COMMUNICATE: To express thoughts, feelings, and actions so they are understood

COMMUNITY: A social group having common interests; similarity or identity among people

COMPROMISE: A settlement of differences in which each side makes concessions

CONFIDENTIAL: Private or secret

CONFLICT: Controversy or disagreement; to come into opposition

CONFRONT: To face with hostility or oppose defiantly

CONSEQUENCE: That which logically or naturally follows an action

CONTROL: To direct, guide, or influence

COOPERATION: Associating for mutual benefit; working toward a common end or purpose

CREATE: To bring into being, originate, or produce

CULTURAL BACKGROUND: A person's ethnic background, income, place of residence, and upbringing

DEESCALATE: To decrease the intensity of

DIFFERENCE: The condition or degree of being unlike, dissimilar, or diverse

DISAGREEMENT: A failure or refusal to agree; a difference of opinion

DISCRIMINATION: An act based on prejudice

DISPUTANT: One engaged in an argument or conflict

DIVERSITY: The fact or quality of being different or distinct

EMOTION: A strong feeling (for example, joy, sorrow, reverence, hate, love)

EMPATHIC: Characterized by understanding so intimate that the feelings, thoughts, and actions of one are easily known by another

ESCALATE: To increase or intensify

ETHNIC: Relating to large groups of people classed according to common racial, national, or cultural background

FREEDOM: The capacity to exercise choice or free will (one of the four basic needs)

FUN: Enjoyment, pleasure, amusement, playful behavior (one of the four basic needs)

GROUND RULE: One of several basic rules for conducting peer mediation, spelled out to disputants at the beginning of the session

HIDDEN INTEREST: In a conflict situation, a basic need or want that people may have that does not appear on the surface to be related to the problem

HOSTILITY: State of being antagonistic; hatred

INTEREST: Involvement or concern; the aspect of something that enables it to matter

INTOLERANCE: Quality or condition of being unable to grant equal freedom of expression; bigotry

MEDIATE: To intervene between two or more disputing parties in order to bring about an agreement

MISUNDERSTANDING: A failure to understand; a disagreement

NEGOTIATE: To discuss with another or others in order to come to terms or reach an agreement

OPTION: Something that may be chosen; an alternative course of action

PASSIVE-AGGRESSION: An indirect expression of one's anger (for example, by refusing to cooperate)

PEER MEDIATION: A process of conflict resolution in which students work together to solve their own problems

PERCEPTION: The process or act of insight, intuition, or knowledge gained through the senses

POSITION: A mental posture or point of view

POWER: The ability to act or perform effectively (one of the four basic needs)

PREJUDICE: An adverse judgment or opinion formed without knowledge or examination of facts; irrational suspicion or hatred for a particular group, race, or religion; the holding of preconceived judgments

RECONCILE: To reestablish friendship between; to settle or resolve

RESOLUTION: A course of action decided upon to solve a problem

RESOURCE: An available supply that can be drawn upon when needed

RESPECT: To feel or show esteem for; to honor

RESPONSIBILITY: Personal accountability or the ability to act without guidance

STEREOTYPE: A mental picture that reflects an oversimplified judgment about something or someone

SUMMARIZE: To restate in a brief, concise form

SYNERGY: Action of two or more people working together to achieve something neither could alone

TRUST: To have confidence in or feel sure of; faith

UNDERSTAND: To perceive and comprehend the nature and significance of; to know and be tolerant or sympathetic toward

VALUE: A principle, standard, or quality considered worthwhile or desirable; to regard highly

VIOLENCE: The abusive or unjust exercise of power; physical force exerted for the purpose of violating, damaging, or abusing

About the Authors

Fred Schrumpf holds master's degrees in both social work and education from the University of Illinois at Urbana-Champaign. He has taught social work at the university level in Idaho and Illinois and is presently employed as a social worker at the Urbana, Illinois, Middle School. He was keynote speaker at the 1988 conference of the Illinois Association of School Social Workers and published a middle school life skills curriculum in 1989. In 1990, he was named Social Worker of the Year by the Illini chapter of the National Association of Social Workers.

Donna Crawford holds a master's degree in special education and an advanced certificate of education in administration from the University of Illinois at Urbana-Champaign. She is presently employed as assistant director of special education for Urbana, Illinois, School District 116. She is certified in Reality Therapy and holds training certificates in mediation from the Justice Center of Atlanta, the Illinois State Board of Education, and Lutheran General Healthcare Systems. In addition to her interests in school mediation, she is a founding partner for Crawford, Kotner & Associates, a private practice providing family mediation services.

H. Chu Usadel left her native New York City to study art at the University of Illinois. She is an award-winning freelance illustrator for commercial advertising, newspapers, and various other publications. In 1988 she volunteered to work a few hours a week with school social worker Fred Schrumpf at the Urbana, Illinois, Middle School. She now works there as a full-time outreach worker in the truancy prevention program, where she designs special alternative education projects for at-risk youth and others. She is the recipient of the 1988–1989 Ba'hai Race Unity Award and the 1989 Honorary Life Membership Award from the Illinois Congress of Parents and Teachers, and has been nominated for the 1990 Outstanding National Volunteer Award.